THE
COURAGE
TO
CARE

THE COURAGE TO CARE

RESCUERS OF JEWS
DURING THE HOLOCAUST

Carol Rittner, R.S.M.
and
Sondra Myers
Editors

NEW YORK UNIVERSITY PRESS
New York and London

Library of Congress Cataloging-in-Publication Data
The Courage to care.
  Includes indexes.
  1. Righteous Gentiles in the Holocaust. 2. World
War, 1939–1945—Jews—Rescue. 3. World War, 1939–
1945—Jews—Rescue—France—Le Chambon-sur-Lignon.
4. Le Chambon-sur-Lignon (France)—Ethnic relations.
I. Rittner, Carol Ann, 1943–   II. Myers, Sondra.
D810.J4C68 1986   940.53′15′03924   86–8764
ISBN 0-8147-7397-4 (alk. paper)

Clothbound editions of New York University Press books are
Smyth-sewn and printed on permanent and durable acid-free paper.

To William J. Flynn,
in Appreciation

CONTENTS

FOREWORD

ELIE WIESEL

In those times there was darkness everywhere. In heaven and on earth, all the gates of compassion seemed to have been closed. The killer killed and the Jews died and the outside world adopted an attitude either of complicity or of indifference. Only a few had the courage to care.

These few men and women were vulnerable, afraid, helpless—what made them different from their fellow citizens? What compelled them to disregard danger and torture—even death—and choose humanity? What moved them to put their lives in jeopardy for the sake of saving one Jewish child, one Jewish mother?

These few evoke our profound respect and wonder. They challenge us to ask ourselves questions. Above all—Why were there so few? Was it that perilous to oppose evil? Was it really impossible to help? Was it really impossible to resist organized, systematized, legalized cruelty and murder by showing concern for the victims, for one victim? Let us remember: What hurts the victim most is not the cruelty of the opppressor but the silence of the bystander.

And what of ourselves? What would we have done? Would we have had the courage to care? Who knows? We can only hope that our humanity would not have forsaken us.

In remembering the Holocaust we must not be numbed by the magnitude of its horrors. We must allow ourselves to be moved by the humanity the victims succeeded in preserving at all times. And we must humbly and gratefully look at these few individuals who, out of their religious beliefs or their humanistic education, with a simple gesture, often acting on impulse, became our protectors—better yet: our allies and friends. Each and every one of them is a reminder of what so many others could have done, of what so many others did not do.

Let us not forget, after all, that there is always a moment when the moral choice is made. Often because of one story or one book or one person, we are able to make a different choice, a choice for humanity, for life. And so we must know these good people who helped Jews during the Holocaust. We must learn from them, and in gratitude and hope, we must remember them.

"Remember that it is easy to save human lives. One did not need to be heroic or crazy to feel pity for an abandoned child. It was enough to open a door, to throw a piece of bread, a shirt, a coin; it was enough to feel compassion... In those times, one climbed to the summit of humanity by simply remaining human."

CAROL RITTNER, R.S.M.

The Holocaust and human decency. Perhaps no two terms could contradict each other more. Most studies of the Holocaust emphasize the abandonment of the Jews by non-Jews who lived under Nazi domination in Europe. It is difficult to do otherwise, for the evidence of human destruction speaks for itself. We cannot minimize or ignore it. During the 41 years since the Nazi death camps were liberated, documents have been collected and books written about the killers, about the victims, about the people who stood on the sidelines and watched without raising a voice in protest as the Jews of Europe were being brutalized and murdered.

We know, however, that during the Holocaust, there were a few people, many of whom were Christians, who could not stand by and do nothing while Jews—friends, neighbors, sometimes total strangers—were persecuted and hunted down. At great risk to themselves they took actions—sometimes large, more often small—which saved a life. Or many lives. And for these actions they are called in Hebrew, *Hasidei Umot HaOlam,* the "Righteous Among the Nations of the World."

In 1953, the Israeli Knesset passed the Martyrs' and Heroes' Remembrance Law which outlined the functions of Yad Vashem, the Martyrs' and Heroes' Remembrance Authority in Jerusalem, and provided a definition, albeit inexact, of the "Righteous Among the Nations of the World." Those people considered worthy of the title are defined as "the high-minded Gentiles who risked their lives to save Jews" during the Holocaust.

Certain criteria, established by Yad Vashem's Commission for the Designation of the Righteous, must be fulfilled before a person can be named as one of the *Hasidei Umot HaOlam.* They are: extending help in saving the life of a Jewish man, woman or child during the Nazi persecution; endangering one's own life; absence of reward, monetary or otherwise; and similar considerations, "which make the rescuer's deeds stand out above and beyond what can be termed ordinary help, which is of course also praiseworthy." To date, about 5,000 men and women have been identified and the accounts of their noble deeds verified. They are honored by Yad Vashem and the Jewish people worldwide as the "Righteous Among the Nations of the World."

In September 1984, Elie Wiesel, noted author, teacher and Chairman of the United States Holocaust Memorial Council in Washington, D.C., convened an international conference, "Faith in Humankind: Rescuers of Jews During the Holocaust." The purpose of the conference was to set forth side by side evidence of human degradation and evidence of human nobility, to illumine the deeds of the few who dared to defy evil at the risk of their own lives, and to bear witness to the world of what was done and could have been done if more people had had the courage to care.

The United States Holocaust Memorial Council wanted to focus on this small but significant chapter of the Holocaust in an effort to discover, if possible, in Elie Wiesel's words, what made these few men and women "different from their fellow citizens? What compelled them to disregard danger and torture—even death—and choose humanity? What moved them to put their lives in jeopardy for the sake of saving one Jewish child, one Jewish mother?"

Surely not every question could be answered, but people did learn that there was and always is an alternative to passive complicity with evil. As Bayard Rustin, the civil rights leader and a member of the United States Holocaust Memorial Council, said at the opening ceremony, "It often took only a small act to save a life. It might have been opening a door, offering a hand, providing a hiding place, feeding a stranger, keeping a secret, or merely saying 'Yes!' Each of these activities seems simple, small," yet forty years ago, they provided a light in the vast darkness that was the Holocaust.

The "Righteous Among the Nations of the World" remind us of what so many people did not know—or forgot—during the Holocaust: that to be human means to care about people who are in danger. They remind us that every person is responsible for his or her actions, and that each one of us can make a difference.

The personal narratives and essays in this book have been collected in an effort to preserve the memory of noble deeds, to bear witness to the world that it was possible to help Jews in Nazi Germany and occupied Europe during World War II. A film, also entitled *The Courage to Care,* complements these first-person oral accounts and reflections by rescuers, survivors, and scholars. Although we cannot help but mourn the overwhelming dearth of "ordinary" human response to the Jews of Europe during the years 1933–45, we also must focus our attention on the few acts of caring and courage, if we are to provide examples of human decency for ourselves and our children.

ACKNOWLEDGMENTS

No project, large or small, is ever completed without the assistance and encouragement of many people. We want to express our thanks to all those who contributed to the team effort that made possible the publication of *The Courage to Care: Rescuers of Jews During the Holocaust*. A few among the many must be singled out for special mention.

The project, "Faith in Humankind: Rescuers of Jews During the Holocaust," which began as the dream of one person, would not have been possible but for the enthusiastic response of Elie Wiesel, Chairman of the United States Holocaust Memorial Council, Washington, D.C. From the moment Mr. Wiesel learned of the idea for a conference, film, and book, he endorsed it wholeheartedly. It is a particular pleasure to thank him as well as the Council for sponsoring the project.

We also want to give special acknowledgment and thanks to Jane Dickler-Lebow. Working with a rough transcript of the conference proceedings, she expeditiously, and with skill and sensitivity, rendered a coherent and readable draft which became the working document for this book.

Professor Leo Goldberger, whose personal account of rescue during the Holocaust is included in this volume, has been a friend and advisor throughout the editing and publication process. His guidance was invaluable.

Kitty Moore, Senior Editor, New York University Press, provided us with just the right amount of all we needed: discipline, editorial comments, wisdom, friendship and humor. She helped us to transform the vast amount of material we had into a readable, coherent book. We are grateful for her enthusiasm and expertise.

During the conference, Robert Gardner interviewed on film several of the people whose stories are included in the book. We thank him for the superb film he eventually produced and directed, *The Courage to Care* (United Way Productions, Alexandria, VA), and also for the thoughtful and caring way he conducted the interviews.

We want to acknowledge the gracious cooperation of Holocaust research centers and archives in Israel, Poland, France, Holland and the United States and their staffs who assisted Robert Gardner, Richard Kaplan, Lynn McDevitt, and Dr. Carol Rittner, R.S.M. as they searched for photographs for both the film and book.

We also want to thank Fran Arre, Marilyn Stern and Lisa Uchno for their assistance in typing, re-typing, transcribing, and assisting in so many ways.

Our families, friends, and colleagues provided the understanding, encouragement and love which gave us the freedom to work full time and more on the project. We thank them.

Finally, we want to thank all those whose stories and reflections comprise the substance of this book: Holocaust survivors, scholars, and most of all, those "quiet heroes" who helped Jews during the Holocaust and whom the Jewish people honor as *Hasidei Umot HaOlam,* the "Righteous Among the Nations of the World."

INTRODUCTION

The
Righteous
Rescuers

IRVING GREENBERG

Each one of the *Hasidei Umot HaOlam*, "Righteous Among the Nations of the World," saved an individual or individuals who were precious and unique, as all people are. The people who saved others also deserve respect for their own uniqueness. One must speak with diffidence of the righteous rescuers; we do not know much about most of them. What we have, mainly, are anecdotal accounts and, truthfully, not many of them. Obviously, there cannot have been a large number of rescuers. We know this is so because the evil forces unleashed in the Holocaust swallowed up many of them; besides, there were so many victories for the other side, the murderers, that there could not have been too many resisters.

Still, one of the most important points to remember is that when a large number or a majority of people came together, as in Denmark or in Le Chambon, they saved not just individuals but thousands. The rescuing bystanders, or the bystanders in general, made the critical difference in the survival of Jews.

The difference in Jewish survival in the various European countries is enormous. It ranged from 95 percent surviving in Denmark to 90 percent dead in Poland, Latvia, and Lithuania. Why the incredible variation in rates of Jewish survival?

Clearly the difference lay not in Jewish behavior, neither in passive nor armed resistance. Armed resistance was a decision how to die, not how to live. Nor was it Nazi behavior that made the crucial difference, because it was murderous everywhere. The single critical difference was the behavior of the bystanders. The more bystanders there were who resisted, the greater was the chance that Jews would survive.

In this introduction, I will present a very general sketch of the Holocaust, not only to allow us to see the Righteous in the proper perspective, but also to give a sense of the context in which their actions occurred and, in a sense, can be measured. The universal destruction is the backdrop against which lifesaving can be appreciated.

The Holocaust can be dated from any of a number of events. I will begin from an obvious point, the Nazi ascent to power in Germany in 1933. The first six years,

3

from 1933 to 1939, was the period of consolidation of Nazi power within Germany. It was also the time in which the seeds for the Holocaust were sown. During this period the Jews of Germany were expelled from the civil service, the army, the schools, and the professions. Jewish professionals, first prohibited only from service to non-Jews, were eventually forbidden even to help Jews, their own community. In this way Jews were isolated. This was an essential and crucial dimension of the Germans' scenario for destroying them: to isolate the Jews, which included exclusion from citizenship, in the notorious Nuremberg Laws of 1935, and additional restrictions on where and how they could live, and move about. There was an attempt to keep these matters quiet, especially during the period of the Olympics in 1936. The goal was to reduce objections to the Nazis' behavior by people outside Germany.

In general, although there was a continuing, growing violence, both legal and physical, against the Jews, it was not completely random. The whole stage is marked by a pattern: First, there would be an attack on Jews, then an extension of the attack, then a pause. And, frequently the pause was used as a time in which the Nazis watched world reaction and gauged whether they could forge ahead or would have to modify their plans. Then, as happened repeatedly, in the absence of significant reaction from the rest of the world, the Nazis would resume the attacks on the Jewish community and engage in further oppression.

People often look back and wonder when the Jews could have been saved. I believe, in retrospect, that the key time they could have been saved was in this very period, 1933–39. As we now know, when Hitler invaded the Rhineland in 1935, even his generals did not believe that he would be able to escape a crushing Allied retaliation. The generals even prepared to attempt overthrowing Hitler in a coup. But when the world let him get away with that triumph, his prestige among the generals soared. This gave him the power base from which to begin to implement his plans for world conquest and for destruction of the Jews.

Often, these plans had a kind of perverted logic, some were even not anti-Semitic in their initial focus. The notorious euthanasia program was originally supposed to be a program to rid Germany of so-called mental defectives. It was begun in a rather tentative way. Gassing, in particular, was tried only as an experiment. The program was stopped for it evoked a series of severe criticism and protests, first from the Catholic bishops and later from Protestant leaders and families.

The euthanasia program was dropped at that point because the government did not enjoy the full confidence of the people. Yet, it turned out that the research done during this time on killing with gas was to be used later in developing the gas chambers in which so many Jews and others were murdered.

Jewish emigration itself shows an interesting pattern. In 1933, when Hitler came to power, German-Jewish emigration soared. Thirty-three thousand left Germany in that year alone as people panicked. Yet although things grew worse, Jewish emigration decreased each year thereafter. Of course, this was, in part, due to the fact that the number of Jews in the population was declining. In addition, some were perhaps able to "adjust" to the new reality, remaining hopeful that Germany— the "true" Germany—would outlast Hitler. Germany was their home, their country, and they were confident that this kind of barbaric thing would not go on indefinitely. After all, had not Jews experienced discrimination and pogroms for centuries, and had they not always managed to survive?

The victorious German troops parading through Holland.

In 1938, this hope, this illusion, came to an end. The violent Kristallnacht of November, 1938, caused a huge leap in emigration. Frantic and desperate, 50 thousand Jews left Germany in late 1938 and early 1939. After that point it was too late; the war cut off the exits—too little room had been made in other countries for Jews who might otherwise have chosen to leave Germany to emigrate to another country.

Exclusion of Jews is an important measure of the world's response to the Nazis. In 1938, there was refugee conference in Evian, France, at which the question of how to deal with the Jews was discussed. The fact that the Allies—or, perhaps one should say, the world powers—came in without a serious refugee acceptance program was taken by the Nazis as a signal that, essentially, the world was sympathetic to their position. Indeed, it was during this period that Hitler made the famous comment that other nations liked to criticize him to make their hands look clean, but that, in fact, they would not accept Jews because they felt the same way about them as he did.

In 1938, Austria was taken over, and in 1939, Czechoslovakia was swallowed by Germany as a part of the consolidation of power. In 1939, with the invasion of Poland by the Germans, all-out war developed, and with it the full-scale war against the Jews. Lucy Dawidowicz has pointed out that while the declaration of war came in September 1939, the "declaration of war" against the Jews had come some eight months earlier. On January 30, 1939, in a speech to the Reichstag, Hitler said, "If international-financed Jewry should succeed once more in plunging the peoples into a world war, then the consequence will not be the Bolshevization of the world and therewith a victory of Jewry, but on the contrary, the destruction of the Jewish race in Europe." (*The War Against The Jews,* Bantam, 1976). I read this quote for many years without appreciating the full horror of it—until I saw Hitler on film, presenting this speech. The most chilling thing about the speech is that when he had finished that sentence, there was a standing ovation in the Reichstag.

According to Lucy Dawidowicz, in Hitler's mind, "War and annihilation of the Jews were interdependent." The disorder of war would provide the cover for unchecked murder of civilians. Within a month's time, Poland surrendered and Russia came in to take over its share, the eastern half of Poland. Millions of Jews fell under German domination, and from 1939 to 1941 there was again a process of attack and consolidation.

During this period the dominant policy was not all-out murder. There were initial atrocities when the Germans first came through but the policy was more understated—murder, yes, but no mass murder. There was also ghettoization, which followed within the year, by October 1940. At first, the ghettos were mostly open and people could move about quite freely even while being forced to live there. One must remember that ghettoization meant poverty for the Jews, who had to leave behind them much of their property, homes, and wealth. In many cases, their bank accounts were frozen. It meant hunger and malnutrition, and slave labor or random seizures for forced labor.

Within that period, the German government incorporated parts of Poland directly into Germany. The central core of Poland (called the General Government) was set aside as an S.S.-controlled zone in which the Germans had total control and domination. During this period there was racial screening of Poles, and so-called Aryan-type children were sent off to Germany. A half million Germans were brought into the places from which Poles had been evacuated or expelled. In short, the atrocities were directed, in part, against the local Polish population, and not against the Jews alone.

Postcard from Mielic, near Krakow, in the "General Gouvernement" area of occupied Poland, dated October 22, 1941. It arrived in the United States two and one half months later on January 9, 1942, heavily censored on both sides.

There was a brief period after the fall of Poland when the Western Front was quiet. In April 1940, the Germans invaded Denmark and Norway, followed in May 1940 by the invasion of the Low Countries, the Netherlands and Belgium. This led to the surrender of France in June. This was the peak of German power. Hitler had planned the invasion of England by September 1940, but that attempt was thwarted by the Royal Air Force in what is now known as the famous Battle of Britain. During the period 1940–41, plans were laid for the invasion of Russia, which was intended to become Hitler's culminating triumph in Europe. Despite

7

the frustration of not conquering England, the conquest of Russia was the first priority in Hitler's mind. During this period of full-scale war, plans were being made for mass murder. Once again, the notion of unrestrained war paved the way for a stepped-up attack on the Jews.

A task force was set up for political administration and special Einsatzgruppen were recruited to carry out the killing orders. The Einsatzgruppen were shooting squads, some three to four thousand men, broken into smaller units—A,B,C, and D—travelling right behind the Germans' front lines in priority transportation and with special status. In many cases, as the German Army pursued its blitzkrieg through Russia, the Jews were trapped and caught. Right behind the front came the killing squads. Typically, the Nazis would go into a village or town, round up the Jews, take them nearby, and shoot them down.

On June 22, 1941, an all-out invasion of Russia was unleashed. This initial attack on Russia was enormously successful. The Russian Army was unprepared. Stalin had ignored the warning signs, and the Russian people, in many cases, were initially restless and disloyal as the Germans rolled through. However, they soon got a taste of German recklessness and ruthlessness. Although German atrocities were primarily directed at murdering every last Jew, they also killed Russians and Poles whom the Nazis considered subhuman because they were Slavs.

During this period the Germans' success in Western Europe had left most countries in one of three basic zones: colonial, command, and S. S. In the colonial zone, the Germans allowed the existing local governments to go on functioning—either because they were allies or because it was more convenient to conquer them and allow the local goverments to rule under Nazi "guidance."

France, Denmark, and Finland are examples of highly integrated prewar states that were allowed to have their own governments, as long as they did not fight the Germans. In the case of Denmark, the government was a popularly chosen government. In the case of France, while the government was installed by the Nazis, it had strong ties to the people. Several less unified prewar states were allowed their own governments because they were allies; these include Croatia (now part of Yugoslavia), Hungary, Romania, Slovakia, and Bulgaria. Although an ally in a different way, Italy also had its own government.

In the second of the zones, the command zone, the Germans replaced the local governments with quislings, or collaborators. They were not popularly chosen representatives, but the Germans did not take over totally. In these countries, including Belgium, Norway, and the Netherlands, the Germans had a somewhat stricter level of control. The people were ruled by indigenous local groups, but under German supervision.

In the third zone, the S. S. zone, the German administration installed itself, abolishing or destroying all local governments and taking complete charge. This was done in Austria before the war. During the war, Latvia, Lithuania, Poland, Estonia, and Serbia—essentially the Eastern European areas—whose populations, being Slavic, were considered lower-grade humans, were taken over. Hitler's whole attitude toward the Slavs, as an inferior "racial" group, rationalized this total dominance for him and his minions.

Eastern Europe had a long-standing record of anti-Semitism. Helen Fein, in her book *Accounting for Genocide* (Free Press, 1979), has noted correctly that where

A Jewish child in Holland during one of the round ups for deportation to the East.

there was higher prewar anti-Semitism and a tighter S. S. grip, the result was a higher level of Jewish victimization. In these countries (although somewhat less directly linked to Jewish survival rates) higher prewar political and social disunity allowed the Germans to use the nation's ethnic tensions against the Jews. This often led to higher rates of victimization because crimes were committed by collaborators or by the Nazis with the compliance by silence of local populations.

The opposite was true in countries in which less control was exercised or which had lower prewar anti-Semitism and greater national unity. In short, both individual and collective responses were factors in the amount of power brought to bear on the side of evil.

At first, in Poland from 1939 to 1941, the destruction of the Jews was essentially slow killing by hunger, disease, and overwork. As time went on, however, the ghettos were closed increasingly more tightly. This cut the Jews off, not only from non-Jewish Poles, but also from their homes, their sources of livelihood, and a great deal more. The closing of the ghettos carried a death penalty, not only for Jews who left the ghetto, but for anyone caught aiding and harboring Jews. Such a policy was announced in November 1941, in Warsaw. And the Einsatzgruppen were extremely successful in killing Jews. Estimates run from a million to a million and a half victims. It is possible to read the statistics in the chilling text of the records of Einsatzgruppen A, which kept a daily head count of deaths—men, women and children—for months on end. What is particularly striking is the percentages of women and children in these groups. Frequently, the men were sent off to labor or were killed immediately, with the women and children left to be finished off by the Einsatzgruppen.

The Nazis discovered that mobilization of the Einsatzgruppen was not the best way to implement the plan for exterminating the Jews. It had several drawbacks: the use of bullets was expensive; it was slow; and it was not without its effect on both the killers and the local population. Even the killers, despite their hardening and their ideology, found week after week of shooting women and children somewhat disturbing—not disturbing enough to stop, but disturbing enough to cause sleepless nights and nightmares, excessive drinking, and different forms of brutalization. Perhaps the very weakness and vulnerability of their victims led to ever greater hostility and sadism in their behavior.

The result was the decision to look for cheaper, more effective, and less personal ways of killing the Jews. This meant bringing in some of the technicians who had been involved in the euthanasia program, as well as experimenting with travelling vans in which carbon monoxide was piped back into the trucks. This was followed by the use of a more potent gas for killing humans and then the construction of gas chambers and the death camps.

Eventually the Nazis put into operation six killing camps: Auschwitz, Treblinka, Sobibor, Chelmno, and Maidanek. All except Chelmno were in the so-called General Government, meaning Polish territory totally controlled by the Nazis.

The Germans began to transport three million people across Europe to their deaths. Raul Hilberg summarizes what was involved in transporting three million Jews: "It meant railway timetables had to be devised, wagons hired, frontier crossing points organized, shunting arrangements (along the tracks) perfected. Whole communities had to be uprooted, first by means of registration, then confinement to special sectors of towns, then deportation to holding camps, and from there regular dispatch to the East." (*The Destruction of the European Jews,* 2nd edition, Holmes and Meier, 1985.)

Tens of thousands, one might say hundreds of thousands, had to be involved in such a process. At every crossing people were standing and watching. At every stop there were people hearing about it from families and relatives, seeing pictures, and yet few when questioned after the war, would concede to having seen what was going on. Deportations went on, relatively unchecked, throughout the period.

German soldiers taunting a Jew in Poland.

By 1942, Allied counterattack had begun: first in Russia, where the winter turned into a nightmare for the Germans, and then in North Africa where the Allies began organizing for their comeback. It is interesting to note that organized armed resistance to the Germans inside Europe did not exist until the Allies began to regain their strength.

When the Warsaw ghetto revolted in 1943, it was the first serious organized armed resistance in Europe. It was not that the Jews were better fighters, but they knew that they were going to die, and they decided to make a choice of how they were going to die. Great numbers of Jews already had been killed. Those who still remained began to buy a few guns and to organize this incredible revolt. Of course, it was a symbolic statement more than anything else, a statement of hope that others would learn from them for the future of Jewish life, at least, by reading about them in the history books.

The degree of Nazi control in various European countries was a major factor in how Jews were treated throughout this period. The classic examples are Denmark and Bulgaria. The Danes, because they were Aryan, and therefore identified in the German mind as the "right" kind of people, and because they agreed to surrender under certain conditions, had their own government. It is interesting to note that their conditions of surrender included, first and foremost, that the government would not tolerate discrimination against the Jews. The second condition was that they would not have a Danish army fighting in the East, and the third condition insured Danish neutrality vis-à-vis the Axis.

Danish insistence that the Jews in their country were Danes and that they would not accept separation led to the now famous rescue of the Jews of Denmark. The Danes' solidarity was remarkable, thus assuring that no individual rescuer would be punished by a fellow citizen. Further, the Nazis were reluctant to attempt to punish an entire nation. This is in contrast to such countries as Poland, where saving a Jew could bring a sentence of death on the individual.

Equally interesting is the Bulgarian situation. Bulgaria was a far less unified and democratic country than Denmark but Bulgaria's sense that native Jews were also Bulgarians was so strong that the government insisted on protecting its own people (in spite of the fact that the same government abandoned "foreign" Jews in newly annexed provinces). The Orthodox Church in Bulgaria played an important role in the decision to help Jews, which only proves one must avoid sweeping generalizations about the churches during the Holocaust.

In fact, in both Bulgaria and Denmark, the churches spoke up in defense of the Jews. In other countries, France, for example, individual churchmen spoke out against what was happening to the Jews. There are many areas where the churches played important roles in preventing the isolation of the Jews. It is equally true, however, that Pope Pius XII did not speak up clearly and publicly. We know too that the Slovakian Church actively supported the mass murderers.

In Belgium, 53 percent of the Jews evaded deportation, thanks to an active resistance in the underground and to the organized activities of the Comité de Defense des Juifs, which was organized as an offshoot of the underground. What is also striking about the connection of Jews and non-Jews is that in both Denmark and Belgium the underground itself often was organized or was brought into active being in response to the Jewish situation. Just as the mass killing of Jews paved the way for the mass killing of others, so the defense of the Jews paved the way for the defense or the resistance of others.

Furthering the cycle of deportation and the growing organization that made it possible was the infamous Wannsee Conference, which was convened to plan the Final Solution, to make sure it was done properly and to bring together those who would carry it out. One of the most chilling dimensions of the Holocaust is the use of bureaucracy and technology by the Nazis. As Himmler said later, they did not hate the Jews. The killing was done purely with sangfroid—and that was the power of it. When you hate people, you get furious, you kill some, and you work off the hatred. But if you can translate murder into rules, regulations,

The Warsaw ghetto.

bureaucracy, technology, it can go on and on and on. The irony is that despite the fact that the Germans were beginning to lose the war in 1943–44 more Jews were being killed in those years than earlier, when the Germans were winning. The major killing of the Jews was done, during the period when the war was turning against the Nazis, a period when resistance was up.

In hindsight, we now know that the failure of the Allies to make any attempt to bomb the railroad lines leading to the death camps, their failure to try to halt the technology of mass death in places like Auschwitz contributed to the "abandonment of the Jews" and to the unrelenting atrocities committed against them. Attempts to save the Jews in concentration camps never got serious priority or serious attention in those quarters where it would have made a significant difference. Indeed, the very first warnings to the Germans that they would be held responsible after the war for their atrocities deliberately omitted mentioning Jews, even though everyone recognized that Jews were the greatest number of those being murdered. It could be argued that the Germans took that as a signal

A Polish deportation. "Some killed. Others helped the killers or made believe they didn't know. The large majority was apathetic, uninvolved, unconcerned, indifferent... Only a few had the courage to care." Elie Wiesel.

that they would be punished for atrocities against non-Jewish civilians, but not for those against the Jewish civilians.

The Allies' failure to confront the uniqueness of Jewish destiny in the Holocaust was a major factor in the successful killing of the six million Jews. When the Jews of America begged the Allies to bomb Auschwitz, they were refused outright. They were told that it was a war to "make the world safe for democracy." One could not ask for a guarantee of a *particular* fate for the Jews.

Several times during the summer of 1944, when the Germans were at the peak of their killing of the Jews, they decided they were spending too much money on their killing. The gas they were using, Zyklon B, was very expensive; therefore the Nazis decided that the supply of gas they were using to kill Jews was to be cut in half. They saved half the money while doubling the time it took for a Jew to die of strangulation in the gas chambers. In the end, they even decided to burn Jewish children in the camps alive rather than waste money on gas. During all the time that this was going on, bombers were flying over Auschwitz on their way to bomb the nearby I.G. Farben synthetic rubber plant, known as Buna. That was an important war target, a priority, but the camps were not.

During the two years when the tide of war was changing, the murderers gave priority to killing Jews and some non-Jews in the camps. We know, for example, that German troop trains were shunted aside, and trains full of Jews were sent through. One of the great all-time technological achievements—the mass murder of totally innocent people—went on unchecked; a war that was being fought to save democracy in general betrayed the most fundamental responsibilities of humanity and democracy.

It is only against this backdrop of horror that one can appreciate the enormous force brought to bear against the Righteous Rescuers, the enormous risks that they took, and the variation in those risks. In recognizing their achievement, we must also be aware that failure to help those who were endangered rests not only on those who were right there and did nothing to hinder the Nazis but also on those who, possessing the power to help on a great scale, found other priorities and other responsibilities.

Irving Greenberg, a member of the United States Holocaust Memorial Council, is a well-known scholar, writer, and lecturer. He is President of the National Jewish Center for Learning and Leadership in New York City.

STORIES
OF RESCUE

ODETTE MEYERS

FRANCE

My parents emigrated from Poland to France. Although they were quite poor, working-class people, they were politically conscious, having left Poland for political reasons in the late 1920s. As an only child, I was fussed over a great deal by my parents and others. I remember that life seemed very busy and cheerful. There were many friends who would come to visit my parents and lots of picnicking. It was a good life, until the war started.

My father joined the army in 1939. Almost immediately, he became a prisoner of war. My mother and I lived in an apartment in Paris where she was an active member of the resistance. Things were very dangerous.

In the beginning of the occupation of Paris, the German soldiers offered the children candy and chocolate, and they tried to be friends with us. But we children were told that the candy was poisonous. I knew it was true because people were disappearing in my world. They were either leaving the country, or they were being deported, or they were taken to a camp. I found the soldiers terrifying. Once, when I was wearing the Star of David on my coat, I saw some drunken German soldiers. Of course, we Jews were always supposed to show our star, but I covered mine with my school bag. They came close—they were laughing—and I felt from them a great sense of brutality and danger. For some reason, they took an old Jewish woman who was walking behind me, and they dragged her by the hair. I don't know why—perhaps because they were drunk, but I remember distinctly that I was terrified.

On July 16, 1942, the Nazis struck, and 13 thousand stateless Jews in Paris were rounded up by the French police and taken into a stadium called the Velodrome d'Hiver. Thousands of people were taken into the sports stadium. When they tried to round up women with their children, some of the women jumped out of their windows. There were 51 suicides of that kind. Mothers jumped out of windows with their children rather than be taken by the police, who took everyone, every Jew: women in labor, old people, dying people—they actually took some dead bodies. Everyone. Men without families were sent directly to

Drancy, while thousands of others, mostly women and children, babies, old people, the dying, and so on, were sent to the Velodrome. They were kept there for seven days. Later, they were sent to detention camps like Pithiviers and Beaune-la-Rolande. Still later, these Jews were sent further east to Auschwitz and Birkenau. Among the 13 thousand Jews arrested in Paris in July 1942 were 4,051 children. If it had not been for the woman who saved me, I would have been number 4,052.

The concierge of our house was a woman named Marie Chotel, whom everyone in the neighborhood loved and affectionately called "Madame Marie." She lived downstairs from us. There was a kind of corridor between her apartment and the front door. One day, at about five o'clock in the morning, she ran up, yanked us out of bed and said, "They are coming for you!" She threw us quickly into her apartment and put us, my mother and me, into a broom closet and closed the door. When we had gotten out of bed, we had grabbed clothing that had the yellow star on it. So while we were in the closet standing up, my mother, for some reason, was trying to unstitch the star.

The search team came in, and Madame Marie immediately, with all her peasant shrewdness, put on a terrific act of being the stereotypical concierge, like the one on postcards and in stories: the local gossip, the perfect French anti-Semite. When she greeted the search team she said, "How wonderful that you are clearing France of all Jews. I'm so honored that you have come here. Please have a glass of wine," and so on.

They kept asking for us, and she exclaimed, "Oh, those Jews. You know how they are. They live in poor places like this, but they all have money. They have gone off to their country home. I can't afford it. But they certainly can." She carried on and on that way, and they believed her. She kept pouring them more wine. At a certain point, one of them got suspicious and said, "You know, lady, if you're not telling the truth, if they are being hidden somewhere, you'll suffer the same fate."

They wanted to go and see the apartment. She said, "Oh, my God, you wouldn't want to see their apartment. You know how Jews are; they're absolutely filthy. French people are very clean. The Germans are very clean. But the Jews, especially the ones from Poland, they're so dirty." She went on and on. She poured more wine, and they stayed put. They didn't go into our apartment. In the meantime, of course, standing there, I had two feelings. One was, "How can she say such terrible things about Jews or about us? My mother is a good housekeeper, everything is clean." On the other hand, my real, strong feeling was, "I am safe." If Madame Marie is taking care of things, she is taking care of things. She had this conviction that I was her charge, and she was going to

Odette Meyers was only seven years old when the Nazis rounded up the French Jews in Paris.

19

protect me. So I figured that she was doing what she had to do.

Madame Marie's husband, who was called "Monsieur Henri" by everyone, was a member of the underground. He was fetched from his job and he came immediately. Monsieur Henri was a big man. I was quite small, only seven. We walked outside. There were German soldiers everywhere. I remember that. He held my hand. I was trembling. My hand was shaking. I remember that there were trucks full of Jews being rounded up, and he told me, "Remember, look at your feet and keep on walking." It was like the refrain to children from the whole occupied Paris, "If anyone calls you don't answer. Don't look up. Don't answer." So we walked like that. Nobody called. And I looked at my feet as we walked. We reached the subway entrance, and I remember a wonderful sense of safety as I went down into the subway. I was saved, and hidden by Catholics, because this man took me to safety.

The subway station was almost deserted, and we had to wait for a metro, a subway train, to take us to the railway station. There we met with other children and a gentile woman who was to accompany us to our hiding place in the country. It was prearranged by the Resistance. It was a liaison between the Jewish women in the Resistance and the Catholics in the Resistance. I ended up in a Catholic village for the duration of the occupation.

If I had not been saved by this man and woman I know precisely what my fate would have been. I would have ended up in the gas chamber at Birkenau. All the children who were taken that day—and 95 percent of the Jewish children in Paris were taken that day—perished. Only 5 percent were saved. The children were all taken into the gas chamber at Birkenau. None survived, so my fate is very clear. I know for certain that helping me, getting me into hiding was a question of saving my life. That is absolutely clear.

Madame Marie had a very simple philosophy. We were Jewish and she did not want to impose her religion on us, but she told me a story. "The heart is like an apartment," she said, "and if it's messy and there is nothing to offer, no food or drink to offer guests, nobody will want to come. But if it's clean and dusted every day, and if it's pretty and there are flowers and food and drink for guests, people will want to come and they will want to stay for dinner. And if it's super nice, God himself will want to come." That was it.

Whenever I would do something wrong, she would put me on a high stool facing the wall, and she would say to me, "I think you have some housework to do." It was my business to figure out how I had messed up my heart in some way. I had to get a broom and dust pan and get to work. That was her philosophy and what she taught me. It has been important all through my life.

Odette Meyers with her mother, a woman active in the Resistance. Her father was a prisoner of war.

20

She was so important to me that even her name, "Marie," meant a great deal to me. When I was living in the Catholic village and had to pass as a Catholic, it was all very bewildering to me; I had so much to learn. I found out that the peasants in that village affectionately called the Virgin Mary, "Madame Marie." It was then that I knew that I would be safe. I figured, "If they have one— a "Madame Marie"—here, then I'm OK!"

During the war Madame Marie helped in all kinds of ways. For anyone who was connected with me and my family she was a protector. She protected my parents and everyone who knew my parents. After a while, there got to be quite a few

"Madame Marie," the concierge in Odette Meyer's apartment building. She awoke Odette and her mother in the early morning to warn them the Nazi search teams had come for them. She hid them in a broom closet in her apartment, and convinced the Germans the family had gone to their country home.

people, partisans and Jews, in our apartment when it was vacant, as it was during the war and while we were in hiding; Madame Marie used it for others as a refuge. She used it at her discretion, which was always correct.

After the war, when we came back to our apartment, we found that our next-door neighbor was gone. While we were living in the apartment, we worried that this young woman would endanger our safety. She was one of those who was a mistress to a German officer, and so it was dangerous when my mother was talking to people in the Resistance or having people come over. When we came back and she was not there, my mother's first question was, "What happened to our neighbor? Did they take her and shave her head?" They were doing such things to women who were with Nazis.

Monsieur Henri was summoned from his job to take Odette Meyers to the metro. German soldiers were everywhere, and M. Henri told her "Look at your feet and keep on walking. If anyone calls you, don't look up, don't answer."

Madame Marie exclaimed, "Oh no, they didn't. They wouldn't dare to touch her. I took care of her; she's safe. She wasn't the one who caused the war. She was a poor young woman who dreamed of having pretty clothes and being taken to the opera by a soldier in uniform. She didn't cause the war. It wasn't her fault. She's OK. Don't you worry." That was her attitude.

Always there is the question of why: Why did the rescuers do it? The rescuers usually say, "It was nothing. Why all the fuss? It was the natural thing." I believe them.

Madame Marie also had that feeling. I really think that for her, as for others, it was absolutely the natural thing. The reason is that even though most of them were so-called "simple people," with little education, they were really the most advanced form of human beings. They were, in a sense, "geniuses."

One of the things that geniuses often do, researchers tell us, is break rules; they break all the rules. I would say that one of the things that saved me was the fact that in thought and action, even in her life-style, this woman broke rules, yet she was a genius at humanity. She was not just a "Righteous Gentile." She was a good person, perhaps one even could say, in an evolutionary sense, an advanced human being.

Madame Marie's background and life were quite unconventional. She was born to an unwed mother in the village of Vanifosse in Lorraine; she didn't have much of a formal education. She started in life, at a very young age, as a chambermaid in a home, then she worked as a waitress, and she ended up being a concierge. She was the concierge in our apartment house in a day when one's life was at the mercy of the concierge. She was the concierge of four floors. Every tenant was her charge. She was somewhat unconventional. For example, she was living out of wedlock and so was involved in breaking various laws of the Church. She didn't go to church too often but she lived a good life, nevertheless. She was a kind of rough and tough, down-to-earth woman, very round, very pleasant, very vigilant, and very protective of her territory. She was not at all sentimental; in fact she was quite the realist. It was very lucky that we came into her territory.

When my parents came to that apartment, they were the only Jews in the building. She sensed that there were anti-Semitic neighbors around them. So, when I was born, perhaps because she was childless and wanted to have a special bond with a baby, she simply declared to all the tenants and everyone in the world that she was my godmother, and that was that. Although she was a Catholic, the Church had nothing to do with it. She functioned, somehow, outside the mainstream, outside the Church. She was my godmother and she didn't let anyone have any doubt about it. No one crossed her. She simply did not allow a single anti-Semitic act toward me and my family on her territory.

I do think that good people, simple people are much more complicated than evil people, which is one reason perhaps why we don't bother with them so much. Madame Marie is not, I think, atypical of rescuers. A lot of people who helped the Jews, who took the risk, were so-called simple people. One theory I have is that because they were not so literate or formally educated, they had to do their own thinking at all times. They didn't follow what was "taught" them; they figured out everything for themselves. They had to think through everything. I think her story about how the heart is like an apartment and how you have to clean it everyday gives a sense of that. One must live and consider and reconsider all the time. She would say, "I think that values are your responsibility, they're not something given from the outside."

I think people like her do more of their own deep thinking, and make their own decisions because they are more outside of that part of society that molds everyone the same way. I think Madame Marie thought with her heart, that was the important thing. And maybe that's why she did what she did for us and for many other people connected with us. Her principles came from making decisions according to her heart, her conscience, her own mind. In every single situation, each time, she did what she had told me to do: to do a dusting and a cleaning of my heart every day, to see to it that everything was all right. She saved not only my life—my physical life—but my spirit also.

There is a Jewish proverb that I love. It says, "If you are in a place where there is no human being, *be* a human being." I think the business of being a full human being takes a lot of energy and a lot of strong thinking, and that you must think things through by yourself, based on your own experience. That's what I learned from Madame Marie.

Odette Meyers in the Catholic village where she lived during the occupation.

Odette Meyers is a survivor of the Holocaust. As a child, she was hidden by Catholics and members of the Resistance in France. She now lives in Berkeley, California, where she is a university professor and a poet. She is in the film, "The Courage to Care."

23

JOHTJE VOS

NETHERLANDS

I was brought up in a very strict Christian home. When my two sisters and I did something wrong, we were severely punished. When we did something right, we didn't hear a word about it, because doing right was considered a normal thing. That's why we still don't think what we did in the war was a big deal. We don't like to be called heroes. Even the words "Righteous Gentile" rub me a bit the wrong way. To be honest, I don't feel very "righteous" and I don't feel very "gentile."

I want to reflect a moment on the various attitudes that people have in the world, because it is a factor that we must consider when we talk about helping Jews during the Nazi occupation of Holland. There were people, Jewish and non-Jewish, who helped, and there were others who did not help. Similarly, there were Jews who wanted to be helped, and there were others who did not want to be helped, who preferred to carry the burden that was put upon them. It is important to keep this in mind.

In Holland before the war, at least in my experience, there was no anti-Semitism. Children were brought up with tolerance and respect for others. Certainly, in my family and my husband's family, we learned that saying something unkind about somebody who had another race, color, creed, nationality, or whatever, was very wrong and disrespectful. And so it came very naturally to us to consider Jews just like us. We thought of them as human beings, just as we were. It was just as simple as that.

Two questions are always asked of us. One is, Why did we help Jews during the war, and the other is, Would we do it again? Now, to the last question, I have a very easy answer. I don't know. I still work ardently for whatever I believe is right. I am on the steering committee of the Catskill Alliance for Peace. I work for Meals on Wheels. I work to help the people of El Salvador. Whatever we think is right, my husband and I work for and try to help. But nowadays, I don't have to risk my life as we did in that time. So it depends on circumstances. Why did we do it then?

24

Well, my husband and I never sat down and discussed it or said, "Let's go help some Jews." It happened. It was a spontaneous reaction, actually. Such things, such responses depend on fate, on the result of your upbringing, your character, on your general love for people, and most of all, on your love for God. And, I would say, there was also a kind of nonchalance and optimism about it. I would say to myself, "Oh, come on, you can do that."

It also helped very much to have a happy marriage, because when you feel

Aart and Johtje Vos (man pointing and woman to his left), their four children. The dark-haired girl is Moana Hilfman and the man to the far left, Kurt Delmonte, both of whom they hid during the war.

strong at home, you can be strong for other people. A lot of people did not have these advantages. I ask myself whether I can blame the people who said, "No, I can't do it." Some of those people lived in very unhappy homes where they quarreled all the time and didn't trust each other.

People also knew that when they helped others, they would endanger the people with whom they lived, as well as the people they were hiding. Some had family members who were very sick and needed help. Some people were in a location where it was absolutely dangerous, say, next door to "quislings," Dutch Nazis. If you were to know the circumstances of all the people who did not help, you might be thankful that some of them didn't get involved. Some believed that it would end in disaster and failure for them, as well as for the people who were hiding. These people lacked self-confidence which, in many instances, blocked their ability to help.

We had a civil occupation (it was not very civilized, but it was civil), and other countries had a military occupation. The military people were not always very much in favor of Hitler or even against the Jews. Some of them just served in the army because they had been drafted and had to serve as soldiers. The people who occupied Holland, however—in the government—were all Nazi people—all

A hole they dug in their garden for protection in air raids. Pictured here are their four children and Moana Hilfman (second from left).

believers in what Hitler was doing, and therefore, they were much more fanatic and much more dangerous. That's why a lot of Dutch people could not do what so many Danes did.

Some Jewish people also had self-defeating attitudes. We once went to Amsterdam, to the ghetto, where I knew somebody, and we addressed a young man, who had a young wife and one child, "Come to us. We have several people in our house and we can fit a few more. It's just a question of a few more mattresses in the living room. So why don't you come to us? We will help you to get there." We were members of the underground and could take care of their transportation. And he said, "No, I can't do that."

We said that we didn't understand why, and he responded, "Because I'm a Jew. This has been imposed by God on our people, and I don't think it's right not to accept this burden. There must be a reason for all this. I have to accept it, and when I am caught and moved to Germany or to a camp, I will accept it without resistance."

And I said, "Well, this is beautiful, courageous, and very high-falutin', but how about your child? She's three years old and she can't judge for herself." He said, "I have to judge for her."

The happy ending to this story is that we got the child, finally, on the last day, about ten minutes before the family was deported. The child was taken by somebody from the underground and brought to us, and she is still like a daughter to us.

This is how it happened. After the Jews were picked up, the Nazis usually brought in electricians, because the houses were often pillaged. The electricians came in to prevent fires by switching off the electricity. One of those electricians was a Dutchman. I don't know who he was, but he was a hero; he went in there with the Germans to switch off the electricity, it was just a job he was forced to do—and he ended up rescuing the child I mentioned.

The young Jewish couple was there with their child. At the last moment the wife said, "We cannot sacrifice our child for our principles," and so the electrician said, "Okay, give the child to me." The child had a broken arm, and it helped, because the electrician put her on the back of his bicycle and said to the Nazis, "I have to bring my child to the doctor." They believed it, and he was able to bring the child to us. He dropped her in our garden and then disappeared. I still would like to find him one day and thank him.

Some people have asked me whether I was ever afraid. Oh, God, yes! I was scared to death. And very near death also. At one point I was in the hands of the Gestapo, my husband was in jail, and the Nazis were doing a lot of house searching. We were hiding 36 people, 32 Jews, and four others who also were being sought by the Gestapo. We had made a tunnel underground from our house to a nature reservation, and when we got a warning or had an inkling that the village was surrounded, they all went in there. They all came through because we had a house in which we could do such things. It was not always easy and often we were frightened, but we were able to help a little bit, and we did it because we believed it was the right thing to do. And that is why we were able to help Jewish people during the Nazi occupation of Holland.

Moana Hilfman, the little Jewish girl from Amsterdam, whom the Vos family hid during the war.

Johtje Vos and her husband, Aart, were involved in the underground effort in Holland to help the Jews. They now live in Woodstock, New York. Both were honored by Yad Vashem.

MARION PRITCHARD

On May 10, 1940, the German Army invaded the Netherlands. The invasion was a surprise. During World War I the Netherlands had managed to maintain its neutrality, and we hoped to be able to do that again. I was living in Nymegen, close to the German border and awoke very early in the morning to the drone of numerous aircraft flying overhead, and Germans on motorcycles lining the street. It was clear that the planes were not engaged in one of their regular raids on England, but that we were being attacked. It was a miracle that the Dutch held out for even five days in view of the overwhelming military superiority of the enemy.

The Germans knew that anti-Semitism would not be acceptable to the vast majority of the Dutch people. After the surrender, the occupation forces instituted a very unsubtle education/propaganda approach, aimed at converting the general population to the Nazi ideology. Obviously it would be much easier to isolate, and then round up and deport the Jews if the majority of the citizens were in favor of this process. I remember a film called "The Eternal Jew." I attended it with a group of friends, some fellow students at the school of social work, some Jewish, some gentile. It was so crude, so scurrilous, that we could not believe anybody would take it seriously, or find it convincing. But the next day one of the gentiles said that she was ashamed to admit that the movie had affected her. That although it strengthened her resolve to oppose the German regime, the film had succeeded in making her see the Jews as "them." And that, of course, was true for all of us, the Germans had driven a wedge in what was one of the most integrated communities in Europe.

Gradually the Germans instituted and carried out the necessary steps to isolate and deport every Jew in the country. They did it in so many seemingly small steps, that it was very difficult to decide when and where to take a stand. One of the early, highly significant measures was the Aryan Attestation: all civil servants had to sign a form stating whether they were Aryans or not. Hindsight is easy; at the time only a few enlightened people recognized the danger and refused to sign. Then followed the other measures: Jews had to live in certain designated areas of the towns they lived in, and the curfew was stricter for them than for the general population. Jews over the age of six had to wear yellow stars on their clothing; Jewish children could not go to school with gentile children; Jews could not practice their professions, use public transportation, hire a taxicab, shop in gentile stores, or go to the beach, the park, the movies, concerts, or museums. The Jewish Committee was instructed by the Germans to publish a daily newspaper in which all these measures were announced, the regular Dutch press was not allowed to print anything about Jewish affairs. And in 1942 the deportations started in earnest.

One morning on my way to school I passed by a small Jewish children's home. The Germans were loading the children, who ranged in age from babies to eight-year-olds, on trucks. They were upset, and crying. When they did not move fast enough the Nazis picked them up, by an arm, a leg, the hair, and threw them into the trucks. To watch grown men treat small children that way—I could not believe my eyes. I found myself literally crying with rage. Two women coming down the street tried to interfere physically. The Germans heaved them into the truck, too. I just sat there on my bicycle, and that was the moment I decided that if there was anything I could do to thwart such atrocities, I would do it.

Some of my friends had similar experiences, and about ten of us, including two Jewish students who decided they did not want to go into hiding, organized very informally for this purpose. We obtained Aryan identity cards for the Jewish students, who, of course, were taking more of a risk than we were. They knew many people who were looking to *onderduiken,* "disappear," as Anne Frank and her family were to do.

We located hiding places, helped people move there, provided food, clothing, and ration cards, and sometimes moral support and relief for the host families. We registered newborn Jewish babies as gentiles (of course there were very few births during these years) and provided medical care when possible.

Then I was asked by two men I knew well—one of whom had become a leader in the Dutch Resistance Movement—to find a place for a friend of theirs, a man with three small children, aged four, two, and two weeks. I could not find an appropriate place and moved out into part of a large house in the country, about twenty miles east of Amsterdam, that belonged to an elderly lady who was a very close friend of my parents. The father, the two boys, and the baby girl moved in and we managed to survive the next two years, until the end of the war. Friends helped take up the floorboards, under the rug, and build a hiding place in case of raids. These did occur with increasing frequency, and one night we had a very narrow escape.

Marion Pritchard. "It did not occur to me," she said, "to do anything other than I did... I think you have a responsibility to yourself to behave decently. We all have memories of times we should have done something and didn't. And it gets in the way the rest of your life."

Four Germans, accompanied by a Dutch Nazi policeman came and searched the house. They did not find the hiding place, but they had learned from experience that sometimes it paid to go back to a house they had already searched, because by then the hidden Jews might have come out of the hiding place. The baby had started to cry, so I let the children out. Then the Dutch policeman came back, alone. I had a small revolver that a friend had given me, but I had never planned to use it. I felt I had no choice except to kill him. I would do it again, under the same circumstances, but it still bothers me, and I still feel that there "should" have been another way. If anybody had really tried to find out how and where

A street in the Jewish ghetto of Amsterdam.

he disappeared, they could have, but the general attitude was that there was one traitor less to worry about. A local undertaker helped dispose of the body, he put it in a coffin with a legitimate body in it. I hope that the dead man's family would have approved.

Was I scared? Of course the answer is "yes." Especially after I had been imprisoned and released. There were times that the fear got the better of me, and I did not do something that I could have. I would rationalize the inaction, feeling it might endanger others, or that I should not run a risk, because what would happen to the three children I was now responsible for, if something happened to me, but I knew when I was rationalizing.

People often ask, Why did I decide to do what I did?

Let me digress for a moment. Some have explored this question, why did some gentiles act, while others stood by. I have been troubled by the tendency to divide the general population during the war into the few "good guys" and the large majority of "bad guys." That seems to me a dangerous oversimplification.

Let me give you two examples, one involving a Dutch family, and one involving German soldiers.

At one point I had to take a Jewish baby to the northeast part of Holland. A good home had been located, and I had been assured that the people there would not

A school for Jewish children in Amsterdam.

change their minds. It was a long, arduous trip, the baby was fretful, and I was exhausted. When I arrived at the station, and found the man I had been instructed to look for, he told me that the house was not available anymore. The family had been betrayed, and arrested. We must have looked very pathetic, because my informant, who initially just seemed anxious to get rid of us, invited me to come with him and rest a while. He even thought his wife might have some milk for the baby. He led me to a small house at the end of the village. It was warm in the house (a great luxury in those days) but they were clearly people of very moderate financial circumstances. I sat down, and immediately fell asleep. When I woke up the woman had changed, fed, and soothed the baby and was explaining to her four or five children that they should pray for me because

31

Mr. Pollak, with two of his children, the family that Marion Pritchard hid in the house outside Amsterdam.

I was a sinner, that I had had this baby out of wedlock, and that my punishment was that they were going to keep the baby, and I would never see it again. The husband walked me back to the station, and apologized, but explained that if curious villagers were to ask the children questions about this new baby in the family, they would be able to tell a convincing story.

Why did they respond? There were many Dutch who sheltered Jews out of their unshakable conviction that this was the Christian thing to do and what God would want. This was a family who responded for that reason. I have heard this view expressed by other Dutch people.

Another example involves some German soldiers. During the winter of 1944–45, food was extremely scarce in the west, and thousands of women and children, and a few men trudged to the farms in Groningen and Friesland to buy or barter or beg some flour, potatoes, or even butter and bacon. I made the trip with my bicycle (by this time without tires), took my flute, and some of the family silver, and was able to obtain what seemed like a wonderful supply of food. The Germans were constantly patrolling the roads, but the main danger point was near Zwolle, where one had to cross a wide river, the Ijssel. There were always many rumors among the people on the road: when it might be safe to cross the bridge, where a rowboat might be located, and how much would be charged to be taken across, etc. That night the story was that it would probably be safe to cross an hour before curfew time. About 40 of us approached the bridge, but we were stopped, searched, and arrested by German soldiers who took us to a building they were using as a command post. We were told that the food was confiscated, but that we would be allowed to leave the next morning.

I had reached the point where I did not care what happened, threw all caution to the winds, and vented the accumulated rage of the previous four years. In spite of attempts of the other people to stop me (they were concerned for my safety), I told the soldiers what I thought of the war, the Germans in general, Hitler in particular, and the concentration camps.

They did not respond at all. The next morning two of them marched me outside and I did not know what to expect. But they returned my bicycle and my supplies, put me on a truck, and drove me over the bridge.

Why? I don't know. We did not talk. But they took a risk, an enormous risk. They had some basic decency left.

The point I want to make is that there were indeed some people who behaved criminally by betraying their Jewish neighbors and thereby sentencing them to death. There were some people who dedicated themselves to actively rescuing as

32

many people as possible. Somewhere in between was the majority, whose actions varied from the minimum decency of at least keeping quiet if they knew where Jews were hidden to finding a way to help them when they were asked.

It did not occur to me to do anything other than I did. After what I had seen outside that children's home, I could not have done anything else. I think you have a responsibility to yourself to behave decently. We all have memories of times we should have done something and didn't. And it gets in the way the rest of your life.

Now, in retrospect, and after reading Alice Miller's excellent book, *For Your Own Good: Hidden Cruelty in Childrearing and the Roots of Violence* (New York: Farrar, Straus, and Giroux, 1983), I believe that courage, integrity, and a capacity for love are neither virtues, nor moral categories, but a consequence of a benign fate, in my own case, parents who listened to me, let me talk, and encouraged in every way the development of my own authentic self. It may be redundant to add that they never used corporal punishment in any form. Being brought up in the Anglican Church was a positive experience for me and imbued me early on with a strong conviction that we are our brothers' keepers. When you truly believe that, you have to behave that way in order to be able to live with yourself.

Lex and Tom Pollak in a photograph taken during the war.

Marion P. van Binsbergen Pritchard was honored by Yad Vashem in 1983 for helping Jews during the occupation of Holland. After the war, she moved to the United States and now lives in Vermont. She is a psychoanalyst, and is in the film, "The Courage to Care."

MAX ROTHSCHILD

I was born in Germany. As a youth, I was active in the movement called in Holland "Palestine Pioneers," young people who trained to go to what was then Palestine as builders and workers.

We young German Jews were put into the concentration camp Buchenwald in 1938. We were liberated from Buchenwald through the grace of the Dutch Queen Wilhelmina, who admitted about two hundred boys and girls into Holland, on the condition that they would work with farmers for further training. Shortly afterwards, of course, the Nazis invaded Holland, and we were caught again.

The question that faced us in the summer of 1942 was whether or not we should go into hiding. It was not a simple question. We were young. We were strong. We felt that we could hold out better than others. We had good contacts through our work—with farmers, with workers, with the non-Jewish population in Holland. But we saw that all the Jewish people were being taken away. Many of us were torn because we felt that it was our duty to go into the camps and help the older people, to help them keep up their morale, to sustain them, to stay with them. This is a point not often discussed.

There were nurses from our own group who were in charge of Jewish mental patients who were among the first to be taken away. These lovely young girls did not want to leave their charges. They went with them to the concentration camp, and they were the first ones to die in the gas chambers. I feel that these women are the real heroes of the war, and I have always wanted an opportunity to put this on the record, because so little has been said about it.

Why were we facing a dilemma about whether or not to go into hiding? I want to point an accusing finger at the Allies. We lived by the radio reports from the BBC, the clandestine radio. We fed on those reports, day by day. We looked to them for guidance. What would they tell us? What instructions would they give us?

In the summer of 1942, I remember distinctly, they had only a few, inane programs about Shakespeare and God knows what else. All that they said about the Nazis was that the war would be over in two or three weeks because Germany was on the verge of collapse. People who remember those times will probably confirm what I have to say. As a result of these optimistic projections, many of us said, "Well, another two or three weeks. Look, if we stuck it out in Buchenwald for four weeks or four months, we can stick it out here for another two or three weeks." There were notices that read, "You are hereby ordered to present yourself for harvest help at such and such a time and at such and such a station." We said to each other, "Let's go with them; let's help with the harvest."

I, myself, was not smart enough to make the decision to go into hiding and join the underground. If it hadn't been for my good wife, who didn't trust the Nazis, and others who convinced me to go underground, I would most likely not be alive today. So with other young Jews, I went into hiding. We were helped, and we went from place to place. We finally ended up in Rotterdam and were liberated there, after having done a few things in the underground ourselves.

What motivated those people who helped Jews, and who were they? I shall perhaps mention that I am a graduate of the Jewish Theological Seminary, that I am a believer, that I am religious. It has influenced how I think about all these things.

Some of the people that helped our people were social democrats; some were religious socialists under the influence of a lady poet—a wonderful woman named Henrietta Roland Holst who wrote a beautiful poem about the suffering of the Jews, a poem that was spread from hand to hand in the underground. Others were pacifists. The friends who saved us, my wife and me, were pacifists and were among those who had been jailed before the war because they had refused to serve in the Dutch Colonial Army.

For many years, we have asked ourselves what moved them to become rescuers. Why did they risk their lives? Why did they hide us? Why did they share their last morsel of food with us? Why did they go through those many days and weeks and months of anxiety—of fear, every second of the day, that they might be betrayed, that they might be killed? I must tell you that many of them lost their lives.

I asked one of them, a man who saved 27 Jews himself, and who now lives in a trailer camp in Canada, why he did it.

He is a simple man; he was a gardener during the war. I said, "Willem, why did you do it?"

He said, "What do you mean, why did I do it? I let nobody step on my toes. And I don't let anybody step on anybody else's toes. I have no philosophy. I don't belong to a church. But when I see injustice done, I do something about it."

The people who helped us were, perhaps, of a more sophisticated kind. They were motivated by the philosophy of pacificism. For them it was a form of passive resistance—nonviolent resistance, if you will. They belonged to a

On May 10, 1940, the Germans invaded Holland.

movement in Holland that was active in settlement houses. Many of them were religious, but the emphasis was on practice, on practical work—work with the underprivileged, educational work, and so on.

In the fall of 1943, my friend, Niek Schouten, the one who saved my wife and me (he was the director of the School of Social Work in Rotterdam for many years), dressed himself and a friend as Gestapo agents. They went on those bicycles with rubber wheels from house to house in a street in Rotterdam where Jews were living, and they said, "We are from the Gestapo, and we have to pick up the children." Then they put the children on the back of their bicycles and prepared to save them. There was one little Jewish boy, a smarty. He said, "I know that you are not from the Gestapo."

And they said, "Will you shut up, or else!"

In this way they were able to save those children and many of us.

We have kept a very close friendship with those people who saved us. Actually, they named one of their children after my wife. They come here. We go there. We have spent all our vacations together with them. Some members of our family are Israelis, so we spend a great deal of time in Israel. We have been their host in Israel many times.

Most of these rescuers consistently have refused to be honored. They cannot understand why they should be quoted, or cited, or given anything like a distinction of some kind or other. They want to forget about what they did during the war and just go on, being our friends and living the way they have always lived. That is their great beauty.

Max Rothschild is a German survivor of the Holocaust. He was aided in his escape from the Gestapo by the Dutch underground. He and his wife now live in New Jersey.

HERMANN GRAEBE
MARIA BOBROW

Hermann Graebe: I am an engineer by profession. In the late 1930s and during the war, I worked for the Josef Jung construction firm of Solingen, Germany, doing mostly housing projects but also, after September 1939, building bunkers on the fortification line on Germany's western border ("West Wall"). The fortification construction was done under the general direction of the Organization Todt. This organization recognized that I had a talent for organizing and supervising people, so when Germany invaded Russia on June 22, 1941, I received a telegram from the Berlin office of the Todt organization instructing me to report to the offices of the Reich Railroad Administration in Lvov. Because Max Jung had persuaded me to remain under contract to the Jung firm, I agreed to try to obtain railroad contracts for the company while I was in the Ukraine.

I arrived in Sdolbonov in September 1941, where I was to open an office and establish regional headquarters for the Jung firm. I needed many people with different skills for work: engineers, draftsmen, laborers, and so forth. I needed a secretary who could speak Polish, Russian, and Ukrainian as well as German. Fortunately, I was able to hire a helpful and cooperative secretary who spoke the four or five languages—Eastern European languages—that I could not speak. Her name was Maria Warchiwker (Bobrow). She was Jewish, and she told me that her husband, along with 150 or 200 other Jewish men, had been killed by an S.S. Einsatzgruppen (mobile killing unit) about four to six weeks earlier.

Maria Bobrow: At the beginning of the war, I was a young woman in Poland with a young husband. Because I was Jewish, we tried to get away when we knew that the Germans were coming. But running away didn't do us much good, because at the time the Germans invaded Russia, we were living in a small town near the border. We knew that it was going to be bad, but we didn't realize how bad it was to become. Five weeks after the Nazis came, my husband was taken and killed with about 250 other Jewish men. He simply was taken from the house, put into jail, gathered with the others around a tremendous pit, shot, and buried. I was stunned. I was in shock. I was alone and I didn't care too much about anything.

A few weeks later I got an order from the Labor Office to report to work at a place near me. It was obligatory for all women from 16 to 65 to work. I gave in my application which said that I knew several languages, among them German. Right away, I was sent to a German firm where Herr Graebe was director. Because I spoke German, he called me into his office and asked me if I could translate documents. I said, "Yes, I can do it." He gave me some technical translations, which I did, and then I started to work there.

I worked with another translator, a Polish woman named Claire, in a very small room. Graebe's desk was on one side, his bed on the other side. There were lots of papers on the floor, and there was a telephone in the room. That was all. Both the Polish woman and I were Jews, and we both wore yellow patches: one yellow one on the front and one yellow one on the back.

Herr Graebe was different. He asked me why I was not teaching in a school (I had been a teacher before the war). I didn't like those questions. I didn't like his behavior—which actually seemed normal—because up until this time, no German acted normal toward us Jews. We expected yelling, throwing out, pushing, and shoving.

One day I came to the office and found a man cleaning there. He told me that in an adjoining city, Rovno, which was a bigger city, there had been an "action," as it was called. In one night, the Germans had killed around 5,000 people, mostly women, children, and elderly. The news had come to him through the milkman. The cleaning man also told me that something strange had happened the night before, and he told me this story.

A carpenter named Franz Rosenzweig, who worked for Herr Graebe, had come in the evening and demanded to see him. Herr Graebe liked this man very much because he always did good work for him at a time when it was difficult to get good workers. The carpenter said that his wife and child and her parents were in Rovno. He had heard that the Germans were going to take some of the Jews out of the city and that they were going to be deported. He wanted to go to Rovno to be with them, but he needed a permission card because Jews were not allowed to leave the city without one. He said that he would go by foot so that he could get to Rovno to join his wife and her family.

Herr Graebe said to him, "Where are they going to be transported? What do you want to go for? You're my best carpenter. It is very hard to get people who know how to do the things that you can do. Why do you want to go? I'll go to Rovno, and I'll pick up your wife and child. Then you can all live here because you have a work permit."

Well, this carpenter was delighted. Herr Graebe got one of the company cars and went to Rovno. He arrived there around nine or ten o'clock, but couldn't get into the city because the soldiers had it sealed off. Although he tried everything, he was not able to get into the city, but he could hear the screams of the people and hear the shots of the Einsatzgruppen. That night he drove back to his office, and the next morning he tried again to get into Rovno, but he again was kept out. When I came to work that morning—by now he was back in his office—he started to yell at me. "Why didn't you tell me?" Herr Graebe screamed. I said, "Tell you what?" He said, "Why didn't you tell me that they were killing Jews?" And I said to him, "I told you that they killed my husband." Graebe said, "Yes, but I didn't believe you when you told me. Now I believe it, because I tried last night to get into Rovno and I couldn't because they were killing the Jews." Of course, I had no answer to that, but I remember that he was so outraged that he stormed out of the room and slammed the door. As much as I didn't have any feelings since my husband was killed by the Germans, I was afraid for my life. And Claire, too, the other translator was afraid.

The next day, when I came to work, Herr Graebe came into the office, closed the door, sat down, and said very calmly, as if the previous day had never existed, that he had been thinking the whole night about what had happened and what he had seen, and he believed that he must do something about it. But he could not do it alone because he did not know the language, so would we help him? To be honest, I didn't think that I would ever again have emotions, but at that point, I think that I saw the light, and so I said, "OK, I will help you."

Hermann Graebe: Through what she told me, what others said also, and what I saw myself, I came to realize and to admit what was happening. So I kept saying to myself, "No more for me. I am from German parents, born in Germany. Why should I participate here in such things? Not me, As much as I can, I will continue to object to that." That was in November 1941.

Then on October 5, 1942, I was an unwilling witness of the massacre in Dubno. I was there because I had a railroad facility to build, and very close to one of our sites was where the "action" took place. My Dubno statement has been printed many times, in many languages, so I shall only tell you briefly about my most vivid memory of what I saw happen. The soldiers made the people undress. Two men instructed them, "Underwear here; shoes over there; outer clothes there." The prisoners, including men, women and children, did it without crying, without an objection.

One of the most terrible things I remember seeing—and that I have reported before—was a father, perhaps in his fifties, with his boy, about as old as my son,

Friedel, was at that time—maybe ten years old—beside him. They were naked, completely naked, waiting for their turn to go into the pit. The boy was crying, and the father was stroking his head. The older man pointed to the sky and talked quietly to the young boy. They went on speaking like that for a while—I could not hear what they said because they were too far away from me—and then it was their turn.

There were other members of the family there, too—the man's wife and an older woman, a white-haired lady who was maybe the grandmother. She was holding and cradling a child, and singing to it softly. Then a soldier screamed for

Jewish men, women, and children rounded up by the Nazis in Warsaw for deportation.

them to move down into the pit. As I was watching this, I heard someone address me by my name in Polish. It was a young woman, about 23, completely naked like the others—I did not recognize her, but perhaps she knew me from my railroad work—and she pointed to herself and said to me, directly to me, "Herr Graebe, 23 years old." She was a beautiful young woman, as was her sister who was there, too. They embraced their father and mother and the grandmother with the child in her arms, and then they went into the pit. I heard ten or twelve shots, and that was the end.

It was the most cruel thing that I have ever seen in my life—and these people raised no objection, they just went into the pit. I think I shall carry that scene directly to my grave. It was quite a bit to see all that, especially the father stroking the head of the boy. The boy cried and the father talked to him and stroked him. How do you explain that? And how do you see such a thing without being stirred into action against whatever or whoever caused it to happen? That is why I kept saying to myself, "Something has to be done. Perhaps I can only do a small portion, but I want to do my share." I had only one child, a boy who at that time was nine or ten years old. I felt that one day he might ask me when the war is over, "Dad, what did you do?" And that struck me. That struck me.

*As others look on,
German soldiers cut
off the beard
of an orthodox Jew
in Poland.*

Maria Bobrow: Herr Graebe was able to help people by employing them for his firm, to do the work he had to get done for the army. It wasn't always easy, but he watched over them, like a Moses watching over his people, and he was able to protect them with work papers, and he always would listen to hear if there was going to be an "action."

At one point, Herr Graebe said that we needed something that would be completely underground, that no one would know about because there were some German men who knew that Graebe had Jews and that he was trying always to protect them. I was a kind of liaison because everything had to go through the switchboard, and so I could know things and then I could tell him if there seemed to be some danger.

There were people who would come to him from he didn't know where, but people who were my friends, coming from the woods, coming from other people's houses, and so on. He didn't know what to do with them, but we picked up these people anyhow—they were like remnants, because by this time there officially were not any more Jews in the Ukraine. And yet they came, and we tried to help them.

Herr Graebe had more than a flock of Jewish families that he was helping. And all of them had admiration, even adoration for him, for he was their only hope. And he cared about all of us. I found out later, much later, that he was helping other Jews who came to him alone all the time for assistance—and that was without any help from me or from my friend Claire. I would meet these people when I traveled, after the war, and they would come up to me and tell me how he helped them.

With us, he helped people on an organized scale, and even then it was never enough. With the others, he did it as they came to him, individually, desperate, often completely alone.

Many times I have been asked, "Why do you think Herr Graebe did it? Why did he help?" Over the years, I have seen many things in him, but I must admit that I could never figure it out. I know that he has a sense of outrage that borders on the holy, and maybe that is it. When he senses a terrible injustice, he does something, even if it means going blindly in the dark. But to be honest, I don't know why he did it. I could never figure it out.

Hermann Graebe: I cannot explain exactly why or how I did these things, but I believe that my mother's influence on me when I was a child has a lot to do with it. My mother was a simple, uneducated person who came from a peasant family, and as a young person worked for doctors and others in Marburg, Germany. She told me, when I was ten or twelve years old, that I should not take advantage of other people's vulnerability.

We children always had the tendency to do some mischief—I would say even harm—to an old Jewish lady. We would ring her doorbell and when she came to the door, we would run away. My mother said to me, "You should never do that. Why did you do that?" And of course I would reply, "Well, because the others did."

She replied firmly, "You are not the other ones. You are my son. Don't ever do it again. If you do, you will hear from me, and you will see what I will do about you. Would you like to be in her shoes?"

"No," I said.

"Then, tell me, why did you do that? Don't ever do that again. That lady has feelings, that lady has a heart, like you, like me. Don't do that again. Jewish people are good people. I learned that when I worked at Marburg an der Lahn."

This was the way my mother influenced me. She said, "Take people as they come—not by profession, not by religion, but by what they are as persons."

All of this from a simple, uneducated woman. Yet, she was educated in the truest sense, and she taught me by word and example what I had to know. I owe her more than I can express, and I am thankful that I was able to share her loving goodness, even in a small way, when it was most needed.

Hermann Graebe was honored by Yad Vashem in 1954 for helping Jews during the Holocaust. As a construction engineer working on projects for the German railroad, he was able to save the lives of more than three hundred Jews in the Ukraine, and in Poland and Germany. He now lives in San Francisco.

Maria (Warchiwker) Bobrow is a Polish-Jewish survivor of the Holocaust. She was helped by Hermann Graebe. She also helped Herr Graebe save the lives of other Jews. Mrs. Bobrow now lives in Florida.

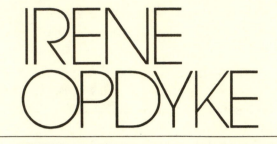

IRENE OPDYKE

POLAND

In my house a Polish girl, a woman, wasn't expected to be involved with politics. We were prepared to be married, to be good wives and good mothers, so I really wasn't affected by political issues or anti-Semitism. Besides, I did not have that in my home.

My mother was just the most wonderful woman, a saint. She was a woman with very little education. When she was only a little girl, her father was killed and she was left to raise her brother and sister. She probably taught me more than anything else to keep my heart, my hands, my ears open for anybody needy. These were her ABCs and she taught them to us. We always had people coming—they were poor, sick—and my mother always knew how to help and what to do to help.

I have often tried to discover in myself what gave me the courage to help Jews during the war. I am sure that it was due to my parents, who always played and prayed together with us children. Although we had a sheltered life, my parents raised me to respect the Ten Commandments and to be at peace with God and people.

I was a 19-year-old student when the war started in 1939. I was happy and proud to have been born in Poland, a free country after 143 years. Maybe that also was the reason I did what I did later: I was Polish, I was proud, I wanted the best. I wanted my parents and my country to be proud of me. That's why I wanted to be a nurse. I was trying to be another Florence Nightingale. I had big ideas: I wanted to go to other countries, I wanted to help. But my dream never got finished because the Germans, without declaring war, invaded Poland. Immediately, I was cut off, separated from my family.

The hospital where I was working and studying started to fill up with wounded and dying people. We tried to help, to save lives, but the Germans were pushing like lightning. In a couple of days, they were almost at the door. The Polish military had to evacuate. Since I could not go home—the Germans were already there—I joined the Polish Army. For days we were on the run. The Germans were pursuing us with unbelievable speed, creating destruction and death everywhere. And in three weeks, with us almost at the Russian border, the war was over. The Polish Army was defeated. I was far from home, and I did not know what to do and where to go. With the remnants of the Polish Army some other nurses and I escaped to a big Ukrainian forest, close to the Russian border. That was the beginning of the Polish underground.

Just before Christmas, a small group of soldiers, a nurse, and I went to the villages and tried to exchange coffee, tobacco, and sugar for something to eat. They left me on guard. I saw them spread around to go to the houses. I heard noise. Before I had a chance to know where it was coming from or what it was, I saw a truck and Russian soldiers jumping off. I ran like a scared little rabbit for the forest. That was the only thing I knew to do, but it was too late. They knocked me down. I was beaten and raped. They left me lying there. When I was found by other Russian soldiers, I was taken to a hospital. And when I came to, I felt two warm arms around my shoulders, and a hand was petting my hair. I thought for a minute that it was a dream, that my mother was there. I looked up and saw a woman doctor speaking a language that I did not understand, but her emotion, her embrace, maybe saved my sanity. She was a Russian doctor who was the head of that hospital.

When I started to feel better, she assigned me to work in the hospital. In 1940 the Russians were fighting the Germans, and she was sent to the front. For me, it was awful because I was assigned to work in a hospital that had infectious diseases—typhus, meningitis—but little medicine, only a little sulphur. But the Lord had other plans for me, so I survived.

In 1941 there was an exchange of Polish population between the Russians and the Germans. I wanted to go back to Poland, which was occupied by the Germans, because I was hoping to find my family. On the way home to Kozlowa Gora, which is three kilometers from the Russian border, I stopped in Radom. I went to church one Sunday. After the mass and other services, the church was surrounded by the Germans, who picked up all the young men and women to send them to Germany to work. Young German men were needed to fight, so the Nazis needed slaves to do their work. But before I was sent with the others, a group of officers came in, and one man, in the uniform of a major, started pointing at random and saying, "this one, this one, this one." I was picked also and by God's miracle, I was not sent to Germany. Instead, I was sent to work in an ammunition factory.

I wanted to work because I was hungry, and I didn't have my parents and family there to care for me. One day, maybe because I had developed anemia, I fainted

Irene Opdyke was nineteen when the Germans invaded Poland. Away from her home, studying, and working in a hospital, she was captured by the Germans and forced to work in a factory in Tarnapol.

45

A German major had asked her to do their laundry. At the laundry, she met twelve Jewish people who became her friends. She is pictured here (on the far left) with two of them soon after the war.

right in front of the whole plant. When I came to, a German, an older man in his late sixties, was standing before me. He asked me what had happened, and I answered him in German. He was very impressed. I told him, "Please forgive me. I want to work, but I am not well." So he said, "OK, you report to another part of the plant and I will give you another job." I was inexperienced and not well educated, but I knew then that the Lord had put me in the right place at the right moment to make that German major notice me. My new job was serving breakfast, lunch, and dinner to the German officers and secretaries, and to the head of the local Gestapo. I started to feel better because the food was good and it was clean. But it was while I was working there that for the first time I realized what was happening to the Jewish people, because behind the hotel there was a ghetto, and I could see for myself.

It was unbelievable to me that any human being could be so mean to others. I saw the people in the ghetto: families, older parents, little children, pregnant women, the crippled, the sick. The Nazis put them all in the ghetto for later disposal. One day, I saw a death march. They pushed the people like cattle through the middle of the town. And the Gestapo was kicking and pushing those who walked too slowly or that were not in line. I saw an old man who looked to me like a rabbi, with a white beard, white hair. He was carrying a Torah. Next to him I saw a beautiful woman in her last months of pregnancy. And next to her I saw another young woman with a little girl holding her skirt with all her might. There were old women, men hobbling on crutches—a long, long procession. Most of all, I remember the children—all sizes, all ages. The little ones screaming, crying, "Mama, Mama," and the bigger ones—they were even too scared to cry. One thing I remember: the eyes—big, scary; looking, searching, as if asking, "What did I do? What did I do?"

We were standing, watching that inhuman march, but what could we do? We were a few women and men standing. There were dozens of Gestapo with guns. Later, I went with someone whose husband was a Jew and saw a nightmare that I will never forget: bodies plowed into a shallow grave. The earth was heaving with the breath of those who were buried alive. It was then that I prayed and promised that I would do whatever I could.

The whole plant was moved to Tarnopol and I was moved with them. I was transferred from factory work and was assigned to serve breakfast, lunch, and dinner for the German officers and secretaries, and also sometimes for the local head of the Gestapo, because I knew German.

I also took care of 12 Jewish people who washed clothes for the Germans. Once they had been people of means. They had been nurses, businessmen, businesswomen, a medical student, a lawyer. Now they had to do that dirty work or die. We became good friends. I didn't have a family. They were persecuted. It was a human bond. That's how I felt. I did not think of them as different because they were Jews. To me, we were all in trouble and we had a common enemy.

We created a grapevine information center. I became the eyes and the ears for the Jewish people. And these 12 would use their footwork to spread the news to other Jews—when there would be unexpected raids on ghettos and so on. We saved many lives because people were warned. Some of them could escape, if they had a place to hide, and some escaped to the forest. There was a place, Janowka, about eight kilometers from Tarnopol.

When the ghetto was liquidated, her twelve Jewish friends had no place to go. Like a miracle, said Irene Opdyke, the German major asked her to live in his villa and be his housekeeper which allowed her to take her Jewish friends and hide them in the cellar.

In Janowka, about three hundred Jewish people escaped. Some of them were from our plant, and some were from other German plants. And all because those 12 Jews were carrying information to the ghetto. (It spread around, you know, to the people.)

There was a priest in Janowka. He knew about the Jews' escape—many of the Polish people knew about it. Can you imagine living underground as the Jews were forced to do when the winter came? Many people brought food and other things—not right to the forest, but to the edge—from the village. The priest could not say directly "help the Jews," but he would say in church, "Not one of you should take the blood of your brother."

When the time came for the total liquidation of the ghetto, those 12 people in my factory did not have a place to go. They asked me for help. What could I do? I, at that time, lived in a tiny little room by the diner. I didn't have a home to take them to. There was only one thing left for me to do. I did not have any resources; I didn't have my parents. I prayed. And as I prayed that night, I threw a tantrum at my Maker: "I do not believe in you! You are a figment of my imagination! How can you allow such a thing to happen?" The next day I was on my knees, saying, "Forgive me. I don't know what I'm talking about. Your will be done."

The next morning, like a miracle, the major asked me to be his housekeeper. He said, "I have a villa. I need a housekeeper. Would you do it?" The decision was made for me. Like a young child, without thinking or preparing anything, I told the 12 Jewish people I knew that I would leave open the window in the villa where the coal chute led to the cellar. One by one, they went there.

The major was an old man. He was sick. I cooked his special dinners for him. He liked me. I was with him for about three years. He wanted to take a man to be there with me also, but I told him I didn't want it. So I pleaded with him. "Please," I said, "I was held by the Russians, I was beaten and raped by Russian soldiers before I was even kissed by a boy." He said, "OK. Fine. We will try it with you alone for a while. Let's wait and see how it goes."

During the next couple of weeks there were posters on every street corner saying, "This is a Jew-free town, and if any one should help an escaped Jew, the sentence is death." About three months after that, in September, I was in town, and all of a sudden the Gestapo were pushing the people from the town to the marketplace there were Polish families being hung with Jewish families that they had helped. We were forced to watch them die, as a warning of what would happen if we befriended a Jew.

When I came home, I locked the door as I always did, but I usually left the key turned in the lock so that if the major would come unexpectedly, he could not open the door. But I was so shaken up that I locked the door, and I pulled out the key. I came in to the kitchen, and there were Ida, Franka, Clara, Miriam—the women came out because that's what they usually did, to help me. I was white like snow, so they asked me what had happened. I said "I don't feel good." I could not tell them. What could they do? We were talking when the door suddenly opened and the major was standing in front of us. I still can see his chin shaking, his eyes glaring with unbelief. We were all frozen like statues. He turned around in silence and walked to his office.

I had to go face him; there was not any other way. He yelled at me. He said, "Irene, how could you do it? I trusted you. I give you such a nice home, protection—why?" I said, "I know only one thing. They're my friends. I had to do it. I did not have a home to take them to, I don't have a family. Forgive me, but I would do it again. Nobody has a right to kill and murder because of religion or race."

One day in September, Irene Opdyke was in town when the Gestapo began pushing people over to the marketplace. "There were Polish families being hung with Jewish families that they had helped. We were forced to watch them die, as a warning of what would happen if you befriended a Jew."

He said, "You know what can happen to you?" I said, "Yes, I know, I just witnessed what can happen." By that time I was crying; I could hardly talk.

Finally he said to me, "Look, I cannot do that to you. I cannot just let you die." And when he said that, believe me, I knelt down, and kissed his hand; not for me, but for those people, not only for the ones in the villa, but for the people in the forest who depended on me. They remained, and they had hope that they could survive.

Then the major had to leave the villa, as the Germans were retreating, but I could not leave the people in the villa because in time of war you never know what's going to happen. It could last another day, a month, two months. One of the women was pregnant. A little Jewish boy was born two months after freedom came.

Just before the war was over we decided that I would take those Jewish people to the forest. I also was helping the partisans in the forest the whole time, in whatever way I could. Three days after I took the Jews to the forest, the Red Army freed us. My Jewish friends were free to make a new life, even though they were broken in spirit and body. I have often wondered how anyone could

The people she hid, in this photograph taken after the war. From left to right: Morris Wilner, Franka Silberman, Henry Weinbaum, Jacob Steiner, Esther Morris, Irene Gut Opdyke, and Moses Steinburger.

continue to live without a family, with their children killed, having lost everything.

When the Russian army rescued us I went with the partisans, and I remained with them until Russia took all of Poland. I was on my way to see my family when I was arrested by the Russians because of my association with the partisans. This time, my Jewish friends helped me, and wrote my story to the historical committee in Krakow. Then I was sent to a displaced persons camp in Germany. Finally, in 1949, just before Christmas, I came to the United States, and now I live in California.

People sometimes ask me what the lesson is from all this. I think it is that we have to teach that we belong all together. That no matter what a person's color, race, religion, or language, we are created by one God, no matter what you call Him. And I think that if there would be less hate, if people would try to understand each other more, there would not be the wars.

I myself realize that when I came to the United States, I put a "Do Not Disturb" sign on my mind. I did not want to talk about the war. I wanted to have a normal life. I wanted to marry. I wanted to have a child. I wanted to create a new family to replace the one that I had lost.

I had tried to forget, to put this experience out of my mind. But in 1975, there was a neo-Nazi organization that started spreading a lie that the Holocaust never happened. That it was only propaganda. Well, that put me on fire. Why? Because I was there. I lived through it, and I realized that it is my duty to tell the truth about what the Nazis and their collaborators did to the Jews, to tell so that those people that died will not have died in vain; to tell so that a new generation will learn the truth. I know I don't speak correctly, that I have an accent. But believe me, I want the new generation to know so that we will not go through another Holocaust.

Irene Gut Opdyke is a Polish Catholic who hid 12 Jews during the German occupation of Poland. She was honored by Yad Vashem in 1982 and is in the movie, "The Courage to Care." She is an interior decorator and lives in southern California.

EMANUEL TANAY

POLAND

I am a survivor of the Nazis' efforts to exterminate the Jews. There were many people who worked diligently to make me suffer and who hoped that I would perish. But, due to my own efforts and the help and courage of a few people who were willing to risk their lives for the sake of my survival, I am alive.

Before the war began in 1939, I lived with my family in a small town not far from Krakow, Poland. My parents were both successful dentists. Our life was comfortable, even upper-middle class. My parents were well educated. We were Jewish, of course, not religious in the traditional sense, quite assimilated, very much a part of the Polish community, something which was not generally true of Jews in Poland. Polish Jews, for the most part, were a separate ethnic group. They looked and dressed differently, didn't speak the Polish language, and, except for a very small, educated segment of the Jewish community, they were easily recognizable as Jews.

Two weeks after Germany invaded Poland on September 1, 1939, all of the country was occupied, but the Germans did not suddenly appear on the scene and say, "We're going to exterminate you." In the beginning, there was no immediate threat to Jews, other than the usual persecution that Jews in Eastern Europe and Poland always faced. There was a gradual increase in the measures of oppression. First, Jews were identified by having to wear an armband with the Star of David on it. They were isolated and put into ghettos, forbidden to work or to buy food. People hoped that the whole evil empire of Nazi Germany was going to collapse, that the powerful countries—France and England, the United States—were going to defeat Germany. It was later that the concentration camps were established. No one ever anticipated that the oppression would last a long time. And no one imagined that the Nazis would go to such extremes as mass killings and death camps.

When my parents finally realized that the ghetto in Miechow was going to be liquidated and that people were going to be deported, they arranged through a friend, Mr. Gadomski, for me to go to a monastery called Mogila on the outskirts of Krakow. No one there knew that I was a Jew except for the prior, who was told that I was a converted Jew. At the time, I was 14, and I was enrolled in the school for educating young men to become priests. I was a seminarian. I remained in that monastery for about a year and a half, until someone denounced me as a Jew.

I remember very distinctly a conversation I had with one of the priests, a man whose name I no longer remember. It was a chance encounter during which he corrected my pronunciation. I knew that he was wrong, that I hadn't mispronounced the word, but the smirk he had on his face made me feel uneasy. Just a week or two before, I had listened to one of his sermons in which he was berating the people for transacting business on Sunday. He said that in the past that it was the Jews who transacted business on Sunday, but, "Thank God, at long last we have gotten rid of them." That same priest was my catechism teacher and I had heard him make other anti-Semitic remarks. I had a kind of intuition, a sense of anxiety. I realized that he suspected something. That very night, instead of sleeping in my room, I hid in the monastery church organ, which had an enormous bellows and where I knew no one could find me. In the middle of the night, the Gestapo came into the monastery and broke down the door to my room. I could hear them. It was then that I ran away from the monastery.

While I was still at the monastery of Mogila, it was my duty to take the mail to the local post office and bring back whatever mail was for the priests. Once a group of Jews was being marched through the village from a nearby camp. One of the Jews, a young boy a year or two older than I was, was from my home-town. When he saw me, he instinctively yelled out, "Hello, Emek." I responded with some obscenity and walked on. There were other occasions when I was in Krakow and someone from my hometown recognized me and addressed me by my real name. Many times, under such circumstances, I jumped off a moving streetcar or a train. Such close calls were very common.

Throughout the war and the German occupation, the Polish population maintained a high degree of solidarity against the Nazis. The prevailing mood, however, was an acceptance of anti-Jewish measures. Many individual Poles who assisted Jews were denounced by neighbors who did not approve of such behavior. It was rare to be denounced for other activities which were punishable by death by the Germans. For example, it was safe to make anti-German jokes, even in public. Occasionally, the Germans would find smuggled goods, and they would threaten people in an effort to find the owner of the contraband. Smuggling homemade vodka and other foodstuffs, even though forbidden, was widespread, but I don't recall a single incident where people who were beaten

Tanay, his father, and his sister, visiting their grandparents in Kielce, before the war.

53

or threatened with execution ever identified the owner of such goods. Hiding Jews, on the other hand, was not one of the transgressions which was viewed by the population as an acceptable—much less desirable—activity. I know of rescuers who were persecuted, even killed by the native population after the war because they had hidden Jews during the Nazi occupation of Poland. Helping Jews to survive was not only dangerous, it was not popular.

In retrospect, I would say that it was very difficult to determine who would help or why, but when I think about it, I would say that having personal contacts and relationships helped. People who might have been anti-Semitic themselves or

Tanay's parents in the resort town of Kry-nice before the war.

who generally might have believed that Jews were bad and evil would help me because they liked me and thought I was nice. For example, Mr. Gadomski, the man who brought me to the monastery, often expressed his profound dislike of Jews. He spent many hours telling me how contrary and despicable Jews were. They did everything backwards: they wrote from right to left, they celebrated Saturday instead of Sunday as the Lord's day. They used a peculiar alphabet, they were dirty, ugly, and when they died they would go to hell. Unlike the prior of the monastery of Mogila, he knew that I was not baptized, and he would constantly try to persuade me to become a Catholic. Despite his anti-Semitism, he risked his life to help me, and he also helped my mother on one or two occasions.

I would say that most people who helped me were personal friends of my family. But that wasn't always the case. Occasionally, I had a chance encounter with a stranger who took a risk and did something that saved me. Once, for example, I was in a village—I didn't have any papers—and I went to make a telephone call. The telephone was in the house of the village elder. There were

Tanay with his mother and sister, in the mountains in the vicinity of the resort town Zakopane in the Tatra mountains, before the war.

partisans in the area, and while I was in the village elder's house, the police came in. They ordered me to raise my hands while they searched my pockets. As they searched me, one policeman looked at the other and said, "You know, this kid looks like a Jew." And I began laughing and said, "You know, that's quite a compliment you made, gentlemen." So they began laughing, too. It was a joke. But then, they realized that I had no documents, which meant that they would have to take me to a nearby town to jail and that would be the end of me. But I protested and said, "No, I live here. I am part of this village. I just forgot my documents, but this is the place where I live."

The village elder—he was like the mayor—was there, and the policemen asked him, "Do you know this kid?" And he said, "Sure, sure I know him. He is the son of so and so." And they said to him, "Well, he has no documents. There will be a fine of 20 zloty," or whatever it was. The village elder said, "Sure, sure, I'll pay it." And he just produced 20 zloty, and that was it.

Here was someone I didn't know, who didn't know who I was or what I was, he

From left: Tanay's sister, his father, his friend Olga, his mother, Mrs. Mila Kobasa and her son, and Tanay. The family was visiting the estate of the Kobasas who had assisted them during the war by hiding his parents briefly between ghetto liquidations.

just helped. I encountered things of that sort: people who would just help. I doubt he knew I was a Jew, although he might have suspected. He probably thought that I was involved with the underground. But, by and large, people who helped me were people with whom I already had some relationship.

It's easy to assume that people who denounced Jews in hiding were evil people. One has to keep in mind that anti-Semitism and hatred of Jews was accepted by most people. It was not unique to denounce Jews because there was a general acceptance of the persecution of the Jews. In addition, if a person helped a Jew in those days and if the Germans found out, the person as well as the Jew got killed.

56

To be a rescuer under those circumstances took a unique person. It took someone who had a deep-seated conviction that he or she had to help. These were not people making choices on reflection. I would say that they simply had to help, because that's the kind of people they were.

Emanuel Tanay, M.D., is a forensic psychiatrist, who was born in Poland. As a young Jewish teenager, he was able to survive the Nazi occupation by hiding in a monastery. Dr. Tanay is in the movie, "The Courage to Care," and lives in Detroit, Michigan.

JOHN WEIDNER

My family was Dutch and Christian. Even when we were quite young, my parents always encouraged us, my sisters and me, to read the Bible and to believe that love was the aim of our lives. My mother and father taught us that Moses got the instruction from God that tells us "to love our neighbors as ourselves." And we also knew from the Bible that Jesus Christ, who was Himself a Jew, had said that the greatest commandment was "to love God and to love your neighbor as yourself." Both at home and at school, our education was directed toward love, compassion, and service to others.

We were taught also that we should be thankful to the Jewish people because the Torah and the revelations of the prophets were transmitted through the ages to us through them. Our teachers reminded us that the Messiah came from the Jewish people. So we had a special respect, a special love for the Jewish people.

As a youngster, I went to the Seventh-Day Adventist college in Collonges, a small French town on the border between France and Switzerland, near Geneva. My father, a Seventh-Day Adventist minister, was the Greek and Latin teacher at the school. After I graduated from high school, I attended the University of Geneva, which was not very far away, in Switzerland. When the Germans invaded France in 1940, I was living in Paris, where, a few years earlier, I had started my own business, although I was officially a Dutch citizen. My older sister, Gabrielle, was the secretary to the head of the Franco-Belgian Union Conference of Seventh-Day Adventists, Pastor Oscar Meyer, and also lived in Paris. My mother and father, by this time, were living in The Hague, where my father was assigned as a Seventh-Day Adventist minister.

Before the Nazis came to Paris, I knew of the persecution of the Jewish people in Germany. I had read Hitler's *Mein Kampf,* and I was aware of the hate and lack of compassion and love that was reflected in the Nazis' concept of life. But I was really shocked when the Nazis took over Holland, invaded France, and started to arrest the Jewish people. I could not believe in what I saw happening, the "inhumanity of man against man."

I remember being in the railroad station in Lyons where I saw a group of Jewish women and children who had been arrested and who were being deported to the east. One woman had a baby in her arms. The baby started to cry and make a lot of noise in the railroad station. The S. S. officer who was in charge ordered the woman to make the baby stop crying, but she could not do it. In a rage, the officer took the baby out of the arms of that woman, smashed the baby on the floor, and crushed its head. We heard the wail of that mother. It was something terrible. And all the while, the S. S. officers stood around laughing.

When I saw such things happening to the Jewish people, it was something so opposed to my concept of life, to all that I was taught to believe that I felt it was my duty in conscience to help these people. Although I did not know at the time all that was happening in the concentration camps, the horrors, I knew that Jews were being arrested and deported and that the Nazis had no respect for their human dignity. It is possible that if I had known more, I would have done more, but I did the best I could.

Sometimes we have a desire to help but we don't know how to do it. I decided, since I knew the area of the French-Swiss border around Collonges so well, that I would try to help Jews and others who were in danger by getting them across the border into Switzerland, which was a neutral country during the war. In the beginning I did it alone, then members of my family and friends began to help, but I knew that we needed more help, if we were going to be successful. Eventually, with others—we became known as "Dutch-Paris"—I organized a network and set up a route that enabled us to bring people from Holland to Belgium, then to France, and on to Geneva, via the Seventh-Day Adventist school in Collonges, which was at the foot of a mountain and not too far from the Swiss border.

During the war, we passed more than a thousand people, mostly Jewish people but also Allied airmen, through our route. It was very dangerous to help Jews, and it was not easy because it was so difficult to travel from one place to another. We had to find safe places along the way where people could sleep for one night or two and also ways to feed them. Then there were other problems: Where could we get false papers? Where could we find money to pay for papers and food? Where would we find people to help us? Could we trust the people we found? A good friend in Switzerland, Dr. W. A. Visser't Hooft, at that time Secretary General of the World Council of Churches in Geneva, knew about our work, and he not only encouraged us, but he helped us, providing money and other kinds of assistance to us as we continued our underground work. In addition, we were able to get money, through Switzerland, from the Dutch government-in-exile in London.

The Seminaire Adventiste du Salève, where Weidner attended school before the war, located in Collonges, a small French town on the border between France and Switzerland, near Geneva.

Gabrielle Weidner, shortly before she was arrested by the Nazis and sent to a concentration camp.

Often, because I knew the area around Collonges so well, I would lead people who were temporarily hidden at the Seventh-Day Adventist school over the mountains and across the border into Switzerland. Sometimes, we would get to the border and there would be many guards patrolling; other times, there was barbed wire to cut before we could get people across. Always it was very dangerous, not just at the border but in other parts of the "Dutch-Paris" network as well. We were always fearful that someone would be arrested and tortured, as would happen, and that the person would break under the torture and reveal names and addresses, which would put other people in danger.

It was not easy, as people knew who were working with us. One day, one of our agents, a woman, was arrested. Unfortunately, she was not able to hold up under the torture, and she gave the names of all the people she knew who were part of our network. In one day, half of the nearly 300 members of the group were arrested and deported to Nazi concentration camps. Forty including my sister, Gabrielle, never came back.

I, myself, was arrested by the Gestapo, beaten, and tortured several times. But I was fortunate because I was able to escape. The last time I was arrested, I escaped the day before I was supposed to be shot. I did so with the help of a compassionate guard who had been impressed by finding a small Bible in my pocket when I was arrested. I climbed out a window in the building where I was being kept, and without being seen by anyone, I dropped three stories to the street. Nothing happened. I did not break my leg or anything, and I was able to rush quickly away. I reached the house of one of my friends, who happened to be a Dutch priest who was a member of "Dutch-Paris." I knocked on the door and he answered. I shall never forget the look on his face when he opened the door. He said, "John, what are you doing here? I was told that you were going to be shot." And I said to him, "Do you want me to go back?"

Eventually, he got me to a member of the French underground, who was able to help me hide until I could leave the city and get to my destination, which this time happened to be London. This trip was at the request of the Allied command, who wanted to know not only about our work with Allied soldiers but also about our work with refugees.

People often ask me what I remember most vividly about the Nazis during the occupation of France. What I particularly remember were their voices. They sounded inhuman, hard. They didn't speak like human beings, or act like human beings. They were a brutal force without brains, without thinking. I also remember their brutality: they beat me with their guns—on my head, in my stomach, all over my body. They had no humanity. The Nazis were force and violence; they would smash and beat you without pity.

Someone told me about an incident in a small village in France which I later visited, Orandour-sur-Glane, which had been occupied by the Nazis. One day because they suspected that explosives were hidden in the village, the German soldiers took all the men and put them up against a wall and shot them. Then they took all the 180 women and children, put them in the Catholic Church, closed the door, and set it on fire. Only one woman from the town succeeded in escaping. It was the woman who later told what had happened in that village.

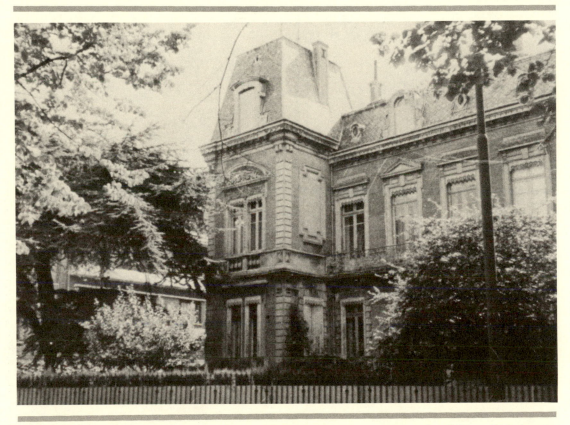

The Milice prison in Toulouse from which Weidner escaped. He jumped from the small window in the third story to the courtyard below.

The Nazis were so cruel, so sadistic. It was not just a matter of soldiers fighting in a war; it was their inhuman way of fighting, and their hatred. You could see the hate in their faces, especially for the Jewish people.

Sometimes I am asked if I have any good memories from the war, and I always tell people that my best memories are of the simple, good people who were

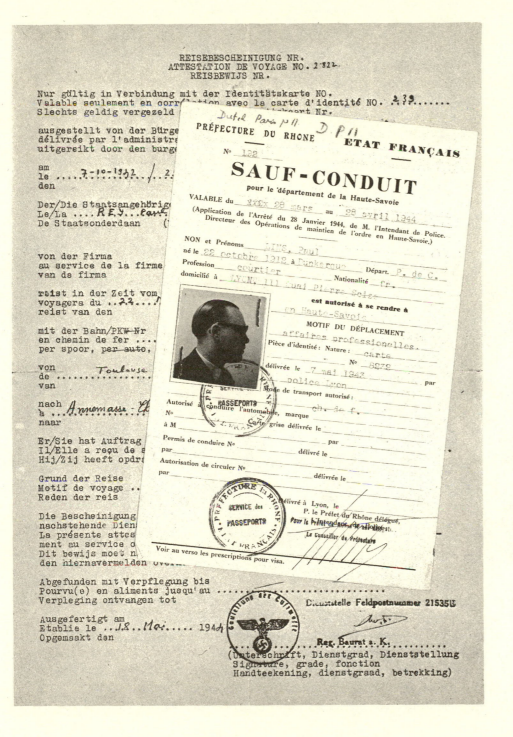

False identity cards, a safe conduct certificate, and Nazi travel permit, all of which Weidner used for wartime travel, with a few of his fourteen different aliases: Jacques Vernet, Paul Lins, and Paul Rey.

ready to risk all, to help, to give shelter, to bring people from one place to another. To see such love and compassion in the heart of people with whom I was working, to see it in all kinds of people, from all different religions, or from no religion at all but who deep in their heart had compassion and love for persecuted Jews, that was most important to me. It taught me that you can have all kinds of theories and all kinds of creeds, but if you do not have love in action, those theories and creeds do not mean anything at all.

Of course there were some people who did not help at all, who perhaps thought that we were crazy for helping Jews. I cannot judge all the people—that would

The maquis check identification papers of people travelling through their district.

be too hard for me to do—but some people were reluctant to help because they had a family and they could not risk it. Others were reluctant because they feared for themselves. Maybe they did not have the courage to take risks. That is something that they will have to answer for themselves. I only know what I had to do, what my conscience and ethics compelled me to do. And I can tell you that I found a lot of people in all kinds of places—small people, of low social position; big people of high social condition; educated and uneducated—who were ready to help because they had pity and love and compassion in their hearts, and who thought, "It is my duty to help the Jews."

During our lives, each of us faces a choice: to think only about yourself, to get as much as you can for yourself, or to think about others, to serve, to be helpful to those who are in need. I believe that it is very important to develop your brains, your knowledge, but it is more important to develop your heart, to have a heart open to the suffering of others.

As for myself, I am just an ordinary person, just someone who wants to help his neighbor. That is the aim of God for me: to think about others, to be unselfish, to learn more and more to be unselfish. I am nothing exceptional. If I have one hero, it is God who has helped me to fulfill my mission, to fulfill my duties, to do what I have to do. But for myself, I am just a simple person. During the war, I did what I think everyone should have done.

John Weidner organized a rescue network in France known as "Dutch-Paris" which helped approximately 800 Jews escape the Nazis. He has been honored by Yad Vashem and now lives in northern California.

Skiing was often Weidner's safest method of travel between remote mountain villages along the French-Swiss border. During the war, he and the other members of Dutch-Paris helped over 1,000 people across the border.

GABY COHEN

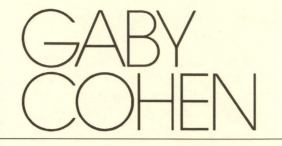

FRANCE

I belong to all those people who do not want to understand how it was possible for the Holocaust to occur. For the last 40 years, I have worked with children, and I have studied the separation of children from their families. Still, it is difficult for me to speak about the four years of the German occupation when I lived and worked with many Jewish children in France. How did they manage to cope with their fears and sorrows? How were they able to endure the forced separation from their mothers and fathers?

France has a very ancient Jewish community. The two oldest groups were the Alsatians, who lived on the German border and in Paris, and the Spanish Jews, who lived in Bordeaux and southern France. At the beginning of World War I, Jews came in great numbers from Eastern Europe, and with the advent of Nazism, many German, Austrian, and some Czechoslovakian Jews arrived in France. By 1940, among the 280 thousand or 300 thousand Jews in France, one-third had come from Central Europe, one-third from Eastern Europe, and the others were Alsatian and Sephardic Jews from the south.

Traditionally, France has been a country of asylum, with a generous open-door policy. On the eve of World War II, France was really the Far West of Europe—you couldn't go any further. It was the last defense line of freedom, the last haven for the people who wanted to leave Europe for South or North America, and the point of departure for those who wanted to leave for Palestine.

My family is an old Alsatian Jewish family. We were ardent patriots, and were naturally concerned about the Jews fleeing from Germany. We knew that the Nazis were especially cruel to them because we had met so many refugees coming through Alsace. But, at the time, strange as it may seem today, we did not realize the full extent of what was going on in Germany.

When the battles began in 1940, my family decided to leave Alsace and go to live with some relatives in a part of central France that was not yet invaded by the Germans. We lived there until late 1942, all the while hearing many rumors that foreign Jews were being arrested and put into internment camps. Some of the stories were quite horrible: people beaten, tortured, sent off to Eastern Europe. All kinds of things were told, but it was still quite vague, and nobody knew exactly what was happening.

After I finished high school, I decided I wanted to become a social worker. But by the time I was ready to begin, it had become difficult for Jews to study in the French universities, so I decided instead to become a Montessori kindergarten teacher. By the time I finished my internship, it was difficult for a Jew to get such a job. So when I heard through other Jewish Girl Scouts like myself about the many foreign refugee Jewish families in the Vichy French internment camps, and when I was told that help was needed in those camps, I decided to try to work in one of them.

I went to OSE (Oeuvre de Secours aux Enfants) which was a Jewish child care agency as well as a medical care agency. I said to them, "Listen, I want to work in one of the camps." And they said, "Well, that's very nice, but we don't need people there right now. We need people rather to help us with children that we are able to get out of the camps." I wasn't very pleased, because I thought that it was much more noble to go into the camps. But they convinced me that it was more important to work with children on the outside.

I played a very small role on this dark stage, but perhaps my story may shed a light on the routine, small horrors our children endured. Maybe it will help us to understand the tears, the anxiety, and the tremendous courage of these children during the occupation of France. What I have to report seems very trivial compared to the sustained and relentless fight led by men and women of courage and commitment who worked to save Jewish children during the war. So many people were part of the effort: Catholic, Protestant, Communist, Left, Right, Jewish, and non-Jewish organizations and individuals. It was really a unique gathering of efforts on behalf of children. American organizations like the Unitarians, the Quakers, and the YWCA fought and fought until they gained authorization to take these children—Jewish children and Spanish refugee children—out of the camps.

When my request to work inside the camps was turned down, I started to work with children outside the camps. In the middle of the war, toward the end of 1942, I was sent to a country mansion in central France, very close to Vichy, about 15 miles away. It was a wonderful place, a peaceful house with trees, a garden and flowers. About a hundred children, from the ages of four to sixteen, lived there. It was a completely new world for me. Each child in this home was carrying stories of unsuccessful flights, half-missed immigration attempts, visas that never arrived, the lost hopes of entire families. These were stories of dispersion, rupture, prisons, sleepless nights, and of a terrible adult game of hide and seek.

In the children's home where I worked, we had very few groups of French Jewish children because the French parents were sure that nobody would ever touch them. Their attitude was, "We are Jews, but we are French. We have been soldiers." Serge and Beate Klarsfeld, who live in Paris and have devoted their lives to tracking down Nazis, have compiled lists of 11 thousand children under the age of 17 who were deported from France. Most of these were children and adolescents who remained with their families, children whose parents did not want to separate from them. This figure also includes about six or seven hundred children who were taken from three institutions in the Paris area that were under the direct supervision of U.G.I.F. (L'Union Générale des Israelites de France), a kind of *Judenrat,* or Jewish Council, set up by the Germans. In comparison, the OSE homes miraculously had very few losses.

For parents, giving up children was traumatic. I spoke with workers both during and after the war, who had brought children to the home where I worked. For parents, to give a baby over to be safe was a most courageous act. Some just couldn't do it, and nobody should judge them. Who knows how any of us would have reacted had we to make the same decision? It has to be said, those parents were very heroic in separating themselves from their children. And some children, too, were very heroic, especially young adolescents who were 14, 15, 16 years of age and did not want to leave their parents. For some of these young people, they thought that they were perhaps cowards in getting out of the camps. They didn't want to leave their parents there. It was difficult, very difficult for the children. Often social workers succeeded in keeping them from getting on the trains, in forcing them out of the camps. It was a terrible task.

Adults can try in some way to fight, but children cannot do anything. Somebody else has to fight for them. It seemed so evident, so obvious that the children had to be saved, but when you saw how much they would insist on staying with their families, it seemed almost an impossible situation. To be honest, we were not as concerned about the future and about the survival of a group, as we were about just trying to help one child or two or three children immediately.

In 1942, Pastor Marc Boegner, the head of the Protestant Church in France, helped to set up an ecumenical group—including representatives from some Jewish organizations—called Le Comité de Nîmes. With the German occupation in November 1942 of the southern zone of France, in which I was living, it became more dangerous for children's homes, where so many foreign Jewish children were gathered. These institutions became easy targets for arrests. If we were to protect them, it became clear in 1943 that we would have to close these institutions progressively and place the children into hiding.

When OSE had to go more underground in its work, activities had to be linked closely with Le Comité de Nîmes and with the Resistance networks. With their help, we began to place the children all over southern France. At the time, none of us young people knew much about these organizations or how they worked. For the protection of everyone the facts were divided among various leaders. I only knew what I needed to know to be able to do my job, so if I were caught by the Germans and questioned, I would be unable to disclose very much.

A camp of young Jewish scouts, located near Tour d'Aubergne, in 1942. Gaby Cohen was in charge of the younger group of scouts, and can be seen here, fourth from the right. When this photograph was taken, most of these children still lived with their parents. They were arrested one year later.

After OSE had to close the children's homes—the work in which I had been very active—I was given false identity papers—actually, I had three sets of papers—and I worked as a conveyor, which meant that I accompanied groups of children in trains from one place to another, often from one hiding place to another. Usually, I was sent to the southern part of France because more of the people there are brown-skinned and dark-haired, as I am.

My papers were not very good. I just had to stick to a story that I was born in a city where the city hall had been bombed and where, consequently, the Germans could not check or control the issuing of false papers. I would be lying if I said today that I hadn't been afraid. All the time I had my toothbrush in my pocket, which was a way of saying that I didn't know how safe I was with my new identity. It was much more difficult for children, who were also given new identities while they were in hiding.

With the help of those in the Resistance movement, Jewish and non-Jewish, we tried to "Aryanize" Jewish children. They were given new names and histories, provided with new papers and ration cards before they were dispersed throughout the country into non-Jewish environments where nobody knew them except perhaps the head of a family here, or a priest or a teacher there. The follow-up and visiting of the children in their new families, schools, farms, or convents where they were hidden was entrusted to non-Jewish workers, either real non-Jewish workers or Jewish workers with non-Jewish identities. The people who did this work most were part of the "circuit Garel," the most important Jewish underground group to take care of hiding children.

For us educators and social workers, the hard task was to convince little children that they were no longer Abram Levin but Alfred Levoisier, not Sarah Weiss but Suzanne Voisin. We had to say, "You, little Frieda Middleberg, you are now Françoise Macomb, or Françoise anything." How could I know whether the child would stick to it? How sure could I be that the child would be emotionally stable enough to answer, "Yes, my name is such and such?"

Sometimes, we spent days and nights just trying to stay ahead of the Nazis. We were constantly rushed and we had to explain over and over again to the children that we didn't know much about the surroundings where they were headed or about the new people with whom they were going to live. Sometimes the child's assumed identity broke down or the child spoke up. When this happened, we had to take the child immediately out of the environment, find another hiding place, and another identity for the little one.

One day I was so upset about a little boy who had already changed his name once before, in order to make it sound less Polish-Jewish and more French-Jewish, and now had to change it again, to make it sound more French-Christian. To comfort me, he said, "Don't worry, I'm getting used to new names." Then all of a sudden he mused, "Maybe nobody remembers my real name." Yes, that also was a serious worry, and at the time, I didn't know at all how things worked, but somehow it was well taken care of and the real names were safeguarded.

One night I was in charge of taking children some place on a train. During the war, traveling in trains was horrible. They were dangerous, the police could enter any time of the day or night and demand to see your papers. We were always frightened because we did not know our lies so well, and besides they were very poor lies and very poor stories, and we didn't know how well they would hold up against questioning. This particular time there was a gentleman sitting in the corner of the compartment and a little old lady. I had only about four or five children in my compartment, there were perhaps four in the next compartment, and four more in another one.

The little old lady was all right—she was sleeping all the time—but I noticed that the man kept looking and looking at us. I didn't know who he was. Was he a Gestapo man, or was it just anybody? Why would he look so much at us? One

This group of boys are in a Jewish scout camp in Chateau Broût-Vernet, in central France, near Vichy. Their parents had been deported and Gaby Cohen was sometimes in charge of this group. Later in the war, in 1943-44, these boys were hidden with non-Jewish families using false names and identities.

little girl with me, whose name was Frieda, and who had red hair and big black eyes, went over smiling to this man. Of course, I wanted her to sleep and just to be quiet, but just then I couldn't say to her, "Be quiet. Sleep." She looked at him and smiled. He seemed very interested in what was going on, and all of a sudden, the man said, "What is your name, little girl with such red hair and black little eyes?" She smiled and turned to me and said, "Nini, which one should I give him? Should I say Françoise or Frieda?" It was terrible. I nearly fainted. I said to myself, "Now it's finished. He'll stop the train at the next station and we'll all be arrested." Such experiences were very disconcerting, because you would feel that all of a sudden everything you had done was lost, you would be arrested and sent who knows where? I was so frightened that I took the whole group and got off the train at the very next station, which was a very bad idea because that gentleman probably wasn't very dangerous. We sat through the night and the following day, waiting for a train which finally arrived.

Eventually, I had to stop convoying children because my Jewish looks became a little too obvious, so I was given a different activity—bringing allowances to families who were hiding children. Often people who took in children did not

This photo, taken in 1943, shows a group of girls who were also hidden in Chateau Broût-Vernet.

have much money, and so OSE had to help them. In France, through cooperation between OSE and the non-Jewish organizations, one found families, Catholic and Protestant, whether or not they had much in the way of money or material goods, who willingly accepted our children.

I do not have a scientific answer for why those who helped did it. I have asked myself that question over and over. For those of us who were young Jewish people at the time, it is not difficult to give an answer as to why we took the risks. We young Jews felt that it was our duty to help the helpless, to help those who were even in more danger than we were. But, for the Catholic and

Protestant families who took risks to help our children, it is not so easy for me to answer why. I believe they were just good people, and I can say that there were hundreds of them, maybe even thousands.

In France, I think the fact that some of the "elite" of the churches—people like the Cardinal of Toulouse, the Archbishop of Lyons, and the head of the Protestant Church—spoke up, also helped. It meant that there were whole organizations that walked with them. But then there were other isolated individuals who were just humanists, just righteous people, who were not afraid to help. On one and the same street you would find a family who could do terrible things; another person who did nothing, who said, "It's a difficult time; I cannot afford to take a risk;" and on the same street, someone who took risks and helped. Who knows? Perhaps it is that if people basically have an ideal—religious, humanitarian, or political—they are more willing to help. Maybe it is a mixture of all of that, I am not sure. What we know is that many people did it, they helped, even though we cannot say why.

Of course much more could have been done in those days on a larger scale by states, nations. But to know that very modest, little people tried to ameliorate our suffering, tried to say, "At least here I will do something. I will move, I will help." That is something, that is a lesson of hope for us all, Jews and non-Jews.

I think of a colleague of mine I knew after the war who worked in children's institutions at the liberation. He was a man who in 1944 had jumped off a deportation train that was carrying arrested members of the Resistance to the camps. About ten or fifteen people miraculously succeeded in jumping from that train. Some already knew at the time how bad things were in Eastern Europe. When that man jumped, he was badly hurt. A farmer found him on the side of the railroad tracks and took him to his farm, where he stayed until the liberation. It was deadly dangerous for these people to hide an underground fighter, and yet they kept him. After the war my colleague remained quite religious, very observant. He worked with children, and they asked him once, "What is an angel? We do not understand what an angel is because we have never seen one." My colleague would tell them—he was thinking of those farmers who had helped him—"An angel is someone who just when you think all is lost, when you think no one will ever help you, that nothing is possible, all of a sudden, an angel is there to help."

Gaby Cohen is a distinguished French social worker. As a Jewish member of the French Resistance, she was involved in helping to hide Jewish children during the war. She now lives in Paris, France.

IVO HERZER

ITALY

I was sixteen in 1941 when I fled with my parents from the capital of Croatia. Croatia was then a satellite fascist state which began a terror against Jews. We escaped initial deportation and tried to reach the Italian occupation zone in Yugoslavia, but we had no knowledge of how the Italians would receive us. We did not know the Italian language, but simply on the blind faith that it would be better than to flee toward the Germans, we tried to cross the border. The train that we were travelling on got stuck, and we were ordered from the train with all the other passengers. We were in a no-win situation: We were stuck in the town of Gospic, where the Croatian fascist movement was born; we had no documents; there was a curfew for the Jews; and there was a concentration camp just outside town.

The situation seemed to be hopeless for us and for the other Jews travelling with us—about 12 or 15 people. But, by chance, a few Italian soldiers who were garrisoned there passed the house where we were staying, and my father, just on intuition, approached them and told them two words. He did not know that much Italian but he said simply, *"Ebrei paura,"* ("Jews fear"). The soldiers immediately reacted and answered, *"Niente paura,"* which means "Fear nothing." Soon, their sergeant arrived. He spoke a little French and told us that he would try to get us on an Italian Army train bound for Italy and thereby, of course, save our lives.

We didn't believe him, but at midnight that night he came with a few soldiers, none of whom we had seen before, who did not demand money or any promises, but escorted us to the railroad station and put us on an Italian Army train. They actually boarded the train with us.

The train was full of Italian soldiers, surprised to see this bunch of 12 or 15 bedraggled civilians running away. But somehow, he was able to explain to them, probably using the words "refugees," "poor people," or even "Jews." I don't know how he did it, I didn't speak Italian at the time, but he managed to get us across the border into the Italian city of Fiume.

But the sergeant didn't stop there. He went to the authorities, asked that we be given food and drink, which was promptly given, and then he took leave. I don't know his name, but I do know that hundreds of Croatian Jews were helped to escape from Croatia, where only death awaited them, into the Italian zone by men like this sergeant.

We were eventually allowed to stay in the Italian zone of occupation, in the town of Cirquenizza. Our representatives, among whom was my father, saw the major who was in charge of civilian affairs very regularly. In fact, seven days after our arrival, the major, hearing that Yom Kippur was fast approaching decided that we must be allowed to observe it. The town was under martial law—you couldn't assemble, and there were curfews—but he called my father and said, "So that you may celebrate your greatest holiday, I have requisitioned a schoolroom. I'm giving you a dispensation as far as our regulations go." He sent a junior officer as his representative, and we celebrated Yom Kippur in October 1941, in a Europe that was burning.

We developed friendly relations with the Italians. My parents played bridge with some Italian officers, and the Italians dated Jewish girls. One would never have guessed from our relationships with the Italian Army that we were on opposing sides.

Ivo Herzer with Hedi Pilis, taken February 5, 1943 in the Kraljevica camp in the Italian town of Porto Re.

But suddenly, one day in November 1942, we were all rounded up and taken to camps. We were taken to the only real camp, a large camp in Porto Re, on the coast. This was a decision taken, from what I can hear or see from the documents, by those in the foreign ministry who were collaborating with the Italian Army on the rescue. They had to stave off the constant German pressure for the extradition of the Jews. They decided to concentrate the Jews, who were spread over a large area, in a few places and to tell the Germans they would examine them to see which might be Italian citizens. (Italian citizens, at that time, were never handed over to the Germans.) That was a convenient excuse to delay things. At the same time, it was undoubtedly easier for the Italian Army to control our destiny by having us concentrated rather than waiting to see what the Croatians would do in one village or another.

Needless to say, we Jews were very shocked. We didn't know the whole story and, of course, we were afraid that the Italians perhaps had been forced to give in, because we sensed that there was pressure. I think the camp had been designed for guerillas and it was anything but a reassuring place. Nevertheless, the camp commandant, in his first speech, assured us that as long as the Italian flag was there, we would be assured that nothing untoward would happen and that everything that we wanted would be done for us for as long as possible.

We organized the camp into a real community. The Italian Army even let us build a hut for our religious services, and Passover services were held there in 1943. We had schools, an elementary school and a full high school. The army furnished the school building and even gave us textbooks. I studied Latin, Italian, and history at the very time trains were rumbling through Europe taking thousands of children to their death. The Italians understood not only that they should not kill us, but that we were in need of recognition as human beings, so they gave us a temple and a school.

Food was scarce, but we were given a small ration. I have a document in which

*A **deportation in Italy***.

the quartermaster general of the Second Army says, "What ration should we give to the Jews? Should we give them the larger one or the smaller one?" Then, the army corps says that since the Jews cannot buy other food (perhaps, he refers to the black market), let's give them the same ration as for the children, that Italian children get. They were always trying to do what they could. Later on, they even allowed us to buy food on our own.

Later, the army took us to the island of Arbe, where there was a large camp. School continued. We even were taken to swim every day under escort—one

76

soldier and two hundred Jews going to swim, and no one wanted to escape. We knew that outside there was death.

Most of the Jews in that camp survived. Some were killed in the mountains with the partisans, and about two hundred people could not be evacuated from the island. They were old and didn't want to move, so they were then seized by the Germans, who came some time in March 1944. Unfortunately, when Italy capitulated, on September 8, 1943, the surrender came too fast. It was a surprise announcement from the Allied headquarters and there was no time to provide for our safety. The Italian Army was in retreat and could not help us, although Tito's partisans came to the island and gave us some respite. It was due to the Italian protection, and the protection of the partisans, that most of us survived.

Ivo Herzer is a Yugoslav Jew who, with his family, was helped by the Italian Army to elude the Nazis. He now lives in Virginia and has dedicated himself to making known the story of how the Italians helped Jews during the Holocaust.

Ivo Herzer, after the liberation.

CHAIM ASA

BULGARIA

My father was the president of the Burgas Jewish community on the Black Sea, which meant that he received all the official mail directed to the Jewish community. In January 1943, he received, in error, a telegram addressed to the commissar of Jewish affairs in Burgas from the commissar of Jewish affairs in Sofia, the person in charge of the commissariat created by the secretary of the interior. The mailman, who was not smart enough to know that there was a commissar of Jewish affairs as well as a president of the Jewish community, gave the telegram to my father because he associated him with Jewish affairs, not anyone else.

My father accepted the telegram, opened, and read it. The message informed all the local commissars for Jewish affairs that they had six weeks to prepare the Jewish community for deportation, or as the telegram put it, "resettlement." The commissars were instructed to prepare lists and send them back to Sofia immediately. Information also was given about train schedules—dates, times, locations—and about how the Bulgarian Jewish community was to be divided into two parts—A and B—so that they could be more efficiently loaded into the trains and transported to the camps.

Of course, he memorized it, then immediately put the telegram back in the envelope and went to the postmaster, who was a personal friend of the family, living on the third floor in our house. (We used to go to his quarters every night so we could listen to the "Voice of London in Bulgaria" at nine o'clock.) The postmaster said, "Ah, those peasants, they don't know how to read. Don't worry, I shall rechannel it." Then he opened the telegram and read it himself. He nearly fainted, then he said to my father, "Asa, did you read this?" My father replied, "Of course not!" But they both knew he was lying.

The postmaster sealed the envelope, re-routed it, sending it on to its proper destination. You might wonder why they didn't just destroy the telegram but they didn't, probably because they viewed it as an official communication and for whatever reason simply felt that one did not do such things. Who knows?

My father immediately made arrangements to take the night train to Sofia and rushed to the *consistoria,* which was the Sephardic equivalent to what we might call today the Jewish federation of each country or the organization of presidents of major Jewish organizations. An emergency meeting of the *consistoria* was called the next morning, and he told them about what he had read in the telegram. The majority reacted by saying, "Oh come on, Asa, that's impossible. This is not Germany. This is not Poland. Such things are not going to happen to us.

In Burgas, the welcoming reception in 1941, when the Bulgarian government appointed a commissar for Jewish Affairs to be in charge of the entire Jewish population of the country. Chaim Asa's father, President of the Burgas Jewish community, is standing in the back row, sixth from the left.

Don't worry about it." And my father said to them, "I'd like to believe what you are saying, but I have read it with my own eyes."

Fortunately, there was another person at the meeting who said, "Look, I've known about this telegram, but I didn't have any proof, so I didn't know how to bring it up, what to say. But now that somebody has seen it—believe me, this is the reality."

The *consistoria* decided to mobilize itself. They organized lobby groups. For six weeks and more, there was intense lobbying of members of parliament (which was still in session), the labor unions, and the Agricultural Union. They decided to go to King Boris III, to contact the metropolitan of the Orthodox Church in Sofia, as well as to canvass ordinary Bulgarian citizens in order to force the Germans to abandon their plans to deport the Jews of Bulgaria.

I would say that the complete answer to who saved and what saved the Jews of Bulgaria is not within our reach. There is no one clear factor to which one can point and say, "This is exactly what happened and why." But let us remember that Bulgaria was the only country where the native, non-Jewish people—the

Chaim Asa's father and stepmother outside of their department store, on June 21, 1941. The sign says, "Magazine (or Store), The Little Elephant, Abraham X. Assa."

proletariat, the simple people—marched in the streets, as they did in Sofia, protesting. This did not happen so much in March 1943 because the deportation of Bulgarian Jews was averted, but it did occur later on that spring, in May. In fact, some non-Jewish people were killed by the police at night during the protests.

The Bulgarians were simple, good-hearted people who refused, up to a point, to go ahead with the edict either from the fascist government of Bulgaria or from the Nazis. And what is remarkable is that they succeeded in preventing the Jews of "Old Bulgaria" from being deported.

While I was not saved individually but as a member of a group, there was a wonderful Christian woman by the name of Marika Karolova who was prepared to hide me if it became necessary. Fortunately, this never came to pass, but several years ago I asked her why she was ready to help me, and she said, in her simple way of speaking: "How could I, as a good Christian, let little Enrico [that was my nickname] go with those people? Who knows where they were going to take him? I was going to keep him; I was going to protect him."

Chaim Asa, now a rabbi in California, is a Bulgarian whose father was the president of the Burgas Jewish community. He and his family survived the Holocaust because of the efforts of non-Jews in Bulgaria.

Chaim Asa, his father, and his stepmother, March 12, 1941.

LEO EITINGER

NORWAY

On October 25, 1942, late in the evening, the telephone rang in the home of Mrs. Sigrid Helliesen Lund, a Norwegian lady known for her activities in the Nansen Committee and with other humanistic, antimilitary organizations. A deep, obviously distorted male voice said, "This is from the police. There will be a large party tomorrow morning, but only the big parcels will be collected." And then the receiver was put down. Party was understood immediately, being a name for the Gestapo action in Norway, while the other details were more enigmatic.

After some deliberation, it became clear that the Gestapo was preparing an action against the Jews and that the "big parcels" were the male adults. This was the start of the rescue operation. Only a few hours remained to get the Jews in Oslo into hiding. The male Jews of Trondheim had already been arrested in other earlier actions.

We don't know precisely how many Norwegians spent the night of October 25, 1942, warning the Jewish families and trying to find hiding places for them. They were fighting an uphill battle. They had little time, and they had to convince persons who did not understand the seriousness of the situation to agree to admit unknown visitors or lodgers in the middle of the night. Those Norwegians who were trying to help Jews also were working against the fact that they were asking non-Jewish people to risk their lives for the Jews, some of whom they probably did not know. In addition, they were faced with many Jews who needed to flee but who did not want to believe that they were really in danger of losing their lives. Of course, the rescuers were also struggling against the police raiding all the Jewish homes.

The action started at five o'clock in the morning and is described in the semi-official history of the illegal transports to Sweden.

It was in Oslo, where eleven hundred of the eighteen hundred Jews in Norway lived, that the main and greatest battle of all was fought between the Nazi persecutors and the rescuers. A month after the arrest of the males, all the women and children were to be arrested. The same warning was given to Mrs.

Lund. This time, the voice said, "The small parcels will be collected, too."

Once again, Norwegians were stumbling around in the streets, and not just because there was a black-out. But this time it was possible to find more helpers. Nevertheless, the rescue operation turned out to be much more complicated. It was, of course, easier to find a hiding place for one single man than for a mother with two or three children. The mothers did not want to leave their half-grown children, and sometimes they panicked. Some had quite unreasonable wishes to take the most superficial and impractical belongings with them. Frightened children were crying and that alone threatened to dissolve the whole rescue action.

A new group of rescuers had been mobilized. A refugee who was a close friend of a doctor and his family by chance had gotten some hints about the impending mass arrest. Forty to fifty people were summoned by the refugee to an emergency meeting in the doctor's flat. Neither the doctor nor his wife knew about it. Even one of the highest leaders of the underground was summoned, and he came. There they divided among themselves the task of warning the Jews, finding hiding places, and transporting people.

All of those present were also ready to take some people into hiding. The father of the leader of the underground, a lawyer, also had several people hidden in his home. Unfortunately, two of them were discovered by German soldiers at the Swedish border when they were to cross. They tried to commit suicide, but one of them was brought to the hospital, revived, and immediately interrogated by the Gestapo. Half in a coma, he gave them the address and the name of the family where they had been hiding. The lawyer was immediatley arrested. Knowing that his son was in a position where his betrayal could destroy a large part of the Resistance, he committed suicide in prison—the same one in which I was a prisoner—on the first night of his arrest. The son managed to escape to Sweden, and, later on, became a professor of medicine. We have been colleagues and good friends for many years, but he has never mentioned the tragedy of his father or the real reason for his death.

There was a Jewish children's home in Norway in which there lived 22 children from Austria and Czechoslovakia. They were brought to Norway in order to give their parents a better chance of finding a country to which they could immigrate. These plans became futile when the Nazis occupied Norway, too, but both the Nansen Committee and the Jewish community in Oslo had to care for the children and kept them in this home.

On the night when all the women and children were to be arrested, a female doctor, a psychiatrist, was alerted by Mrs. Lund, who had received the message about the parcels. The doctor had permission to drive a car, even during an air raid alarm. She immediately came to the children's home. Single-handedly, she evacuated all the children, hiding some under a blanket in the rear of her car. She had to drive four times to the children's home and to the hiding places, but she managed to rescue all of them.

Nine hundred thirty Jews were rescued and during the following months were brought to Sweden—sometimes under the most unbelievable difficulties and

Oslo's most famous street during the German occupation.

despite the most astounding complications. Among those who rendered the most noble services were the so-called frontier pilots, who helped bring people into safety. I have known the lady psychiatrist and many others of the rescuers for years, but they have never mentioned anything about their tremendous achievements during the months of October and November 1942. In spite of their efforts, however, 600 Norwegian Jews and 120 refugees were deported. Among these, only 11 of the Norwegian-born returned. Fourteen of the Jewish refugees in

Norway also happened to survive their stay in Auschwitz, and some of them returned to Norway. I was among them.

There is one small story that is important in order to give a little impression of what it could mean to be a rescuer in Norway. Mrs. K. and her little daughter, aged four, were to be saved. The father had already been arrested. First, they were brought out of Trondheim, the second of the two Jewish communities in Norway, to a small, remote village. But even there, they were not in safety, and on November 29, 1942, they were moved to an isolated summer farm inhabited only by cattle and a dairywoman during the three or four summer months.

The distance from the farm to the Swedish border was about 150 kilometers; the greatest part of the trip had to be done on skis. But Mrs. K. was not Norwegian-born and did not know skiing.

The two young peasants who had brought them to the farm devoted all of their time to caring for Mrs. K. and her daughter. The young men had to go to the village at least once a week to get food. This was not an easy task—not only because of people's curiosity, but also because it was illegal, for all kinds of food were rationed.

The two young peasants started to train Mrs. K. to ski. They prepared a special rucksack made of fur for the little girl. They knew that the mother would never be able to make it on skis alone, and therefore prepared a sort of collar for one of the persons to lead Mrs. K. The other one trained the child to get used to sitting in the rucksack of fur, and he also trained himself to carry her and to be able to help her in all possible situations. In addition to all that, they had to prepare an escape route. After about a month, they decided to make an attempt to get to the Swedish border. They succeeded in their mission, and two days later the two Norwegian boys returned to Norway.

Leo Eitinger, M.D., a scholar and author, is professor of psychiatry at the University of Oslo. He is a survivor of the Holocaust.

This account was largely based on the following two sources: Jahn Otto Johansen. *Det hendte også her. [It happened also here]. Oslo, 1984. Ragnar Ulstein. Svensketrafikken. [The Traffic to Sweden] Oslo, 1974. The author acknowledges them with gratitude.*

JØRGEN KIELER

DENMARK

The German invasion of April 1940 left the Danish people in a paralyzing state of despair, frustration, anger, and shame. These were feelings that continued for nearly a year, into 1941. One must understand that Denmark was a split country which had not yet recovered from the economic and social problems of the thirties. On top of that was the Nazi occupation which meant, of course, that Denmark had lost its freedom.

In 1941, we Danes experienced a national reunion of political parties and social groups, all of whom gradually realized their common cultural heritage and their common goal: national independence and democracy. Nazi sympathizers remained, but they were a very small and despised minority. The national reunion triggered numerous meetings, during which Danish cultural traditions, literature, and national songs were recognized as a treasure belonging to all Danes.

By 1942, however, the Danish international position became an issue of increasing importance. The shame aroused by the surrender of Denmark without significant resistance in April 1940 was still alive. An active resistance movement was born. It soon became clear that the Danish people were divided once more, this time between a large majority group preferring passive resistance and a small but growing group of men and women who wanted so-called Norwegian conditions, or an active fight against the Germans. The goal was the same for both groups: national independence and democracy, but the means were different. It was not only a question of strategy or courage, but it was also a question of ethics. "What will you do, if the Gestapo enters into the room to shoot your younger brother?" was my question to one of my sisters. "Protect him with my body, but I will not carry arms," was the bold answer. In 1942 we were still waiting to see what was going to happen and so the discussion continued.

In spite of all the pacifism among the Danish people, the group to which I belonged, and many other groups as well, started to accumulate weapons. During the spring of 1943, active resistance, including sabotage, riots, and strikes, together with a rapidly growing illegal press, succeeded in creating "Norwegian conditions" in Denmark. The Danish government resigned on the 29th of August 1943, and the Germans took over.

This was a victory for the Resistance Movement, but it did not mean that the Danish people were united, and it is very likely that the discussion concerning active versus passive resistance would have continued if it had not been for two serious German mistakes.

In the middle of September the first execution of a Danish saboteur took place. Nobody could be in doubt any longer that participation in active resistance implied willingness to risk one's own life. Were the supporters of passive resistance willing to make a similar sacrifice?

They got an opportunity to answer that question about two weeks later, when the Germans made their second blunder. They started the persecution of Danish Jews.* It was the opportunity to "protect your younger brother with your own body." The opportunity was seized by numerous people who had been living in an ethical conflict with themselves for several months.

I shared a three-room apartment in the center of Copenhagen with my brother and two of my sisters. We were all students from a provincial town in Jutland. Our apartment was the meeting place of a group of students and naval cadets. It was also a printing office for the illegal press, and it soon became a depot for guns taken from the Germans or from the Danish Navy headquarters. For months we had been discussing active versus passive resistance. With the seizure of the Jews, this discussion was suddenly brought to an end.

Weapons, however, were not enough to save Jews. We needed money and ships to carry the refugees to Sweden. The financial problems were solved within 48 hours. Klaus, a young member of our group, was well acquainted with most of the larger estates in the surroundings of Copenhagen. Together with Elsebet, one of my sisters, he made a weekend trip to these places, and when they returned, they had one million crowns, a considerable fortune. Additional funds were raised by other members of our group, and many refugees also were able to make signifcant contributions.

Through their personal contacts, two young girls, Ebba and Henny, who had joined our group, got in touch with several fishermen and the crew of a small supply ship which made daily tours to a lighthouse in the middle of the sound

---

*This move caught the Danish population in the middle of its endless discussion concerning the moral issue of violence. Now all those who were in favor of passive resistance were ready to prove that their morality was of the same quality as those who were willing to sacrifice their lives.

between Denmark and Sweden. In this way, we established two important escape routes from Copenhagen. Finding Jews, bringing them to the harbor, and organizing and protecting their embarkation became our most important tasks during the following weeks. Ebba and Henny were always there to see them on board. About 1,500 persons were rescued via these two routes, without the loss of a single life.

We did, however, lose one of our friends, Cato Bakmann. Cato was a medical student who did not want to become a saboteur, but he was not afraid to risk his life in the service of the illegal press and the rescue organizations. One day he was surprised by the Gestapo in an apartment belonging to a surgeon at the

Copenhagen during the war. Kieler shared a three-room apartment in the center of Copenhagen with his brother and two of his sisters. The apartment was the meeting place of a group of students and naval cadets, an underground printing office, and a depot for guns taken from the Germans or from the Danish Navy headquarters.

Bispebjerg Hospital. He jumped out the window from the second floor but was hit by German bullets. Severely wounded, he was taken to the emergency room of the hospital, where he died in the arms of the nurse on duty. She was his wife. They had married a few weeks before. She buried her young husband and continued his work.

The transportation of the Jews took about two weeks, but the resistance groups continued even after the Jews were safe. Instead of Jews, we began to transport spies, agents, weapons , and secret material across the sound. No longer did people in the resistance groups discuss the question of passive versus active resistance, for it had become imperative to engage actively in resistance.

There are several reasons for the successful rescue of Danish Jews. Most important is of course the well known warning by Georg Duckwitz, the German attaché, who deserves more credit than any one single person for alerting us Danes to the impending action against the Jews. Nearby neutral Sweden, separated from Denmark by the narrow waters, was another important factor. The inability of the German Navy to supervise the long Danish coastline also played a role, and internal German disagreements were of great help. The rivalry between the German high commissioner, Werner Best, and the head of the German Army in Denmark, General von Haneken, made the persecution inefficient. While these were important factors, the reaction of the Danish people was a decisive factor. In my opinion, the discussion concerning passive versus active resistance represents a background offering a reasonable psychological explanation for this reaction, but a traditional humanistic attitude to life and the absence of serious anti-Semitism in Denmark played their part too.

Many of us came from the organized Resistance, but others came spontaneously when they were needed. National independence and democracy were our common goals, but the persecution of the Jews added a new and overwhelming dimension to the fight against Hitler: human rights. Our responsibility toward and our respect for the individual human being became the primary goals of the struggle, a struggle which required a maximum of moral and physical strength from the rescuer and the rescued alike, and above all from those who were caught by the Germans.

When the stream of refugees ceased, our group continued the sabotage without further ethical discussions. After about four months and 25 actions, some of which represented significant blows to the war industry, the group was finally broken up by the Germans. After the war, we were able to discover that two in our group had been shot in action, two had committed suicide, two were executed after torture, and two had died in a concentration camp. Four survived deportation and others survived underground in Denmark or as refugees in Sweden. This was the price to be paid in order to pursue our common goals. I am not sure that the Danish Resistance Movement would have gained the strength which it actually did had it not been for the inspiration we received from the Jews. Jews don't owe us gratitude; rather, we owe each other mutual friendship.

Jørgen Kieler, M.D., president of the Freedom Foundation in Copenhagen, Denmark, was active in the Danish Resistance Movement during the German occupation of Denmark.

LEO GOLDBERGER

DENMARK

I will never forget it. It is still as vivid in my memory as if it were yesterday. The moments of unspeakable terror as well as the kind and warm social support network of the Danes, friends and strangers alike.

I had just had my Bar Mitzvah in June of 1943. Though the luncheon celebration that followed my performance in the synagogue was not as sumptuous as that of my older brother's two years earlier, it was nevertheless a happy event. I even received a few fountain pens, some religious books and a shiny large police flashlight. To finally become a "man!" Now perhaps I could do some real resistance work in the underground—not just engage in our childish form of anti-German sentiment: wearing a red, white and blue lapel pin, pinching a German soldier in a crowded street then running like the devil, or pouring sugar in the gas tank of a German car, and the like.

With my parents and two brothers we had moved in 1934 to Denmark from Troppau (in the Moravian part of Czechoslovakia) where my father had been serving as chief cantor. (He and my mother had originally come from Bratislava, Slovakia, and after a few years in Yugoslavia, where I was born, had settled in Troppau, a prosperous and comfortable Jewish community.) Albeit a restless person, my father had sensed anti-Semitism in the air and cast about for a new position and a new country. It may have been a Nazi parade here and a German nationalistic slogan there, not to mention direct anti-Semitic remarks which made my father want out, despite all assurances by his many friends and fellow Jews in Troppau that he was imagining things. By chance, really, there was a vacancy for the prestigious cantorial position in Copenhagen's Great Synagogue. He applied, tried out for it and was appointed. Moving—furniture, grand piano and all—we quickly were settled in the picturesque old center of town, integrated into the cozy Danish way of life, learned the language and its customs and felt very much at home there. There was nary a hint of anti-Semitism. Jews had achieved their full civil rights way back in 1814, generations ago, and had over the years earned a highly respected place in all walks of life.

90

Then came the fateful day. April 9, 1940. The widening scope of the war hit our beautiful, little, and avowedly neutral land—after it has only recently signed an antiaggression pact with the Germans. The early morning sky was blackened by roaring low-flying planes. From my window I reached out to catch a green leaflet coming down from the sky like confetti. In comical, broken Danish the leaflet appealed to all Danes to remain calm. The German *Wehrmacht* had no aggressive intentions, they only wanted to protect us from the evil designs of the Allies. We were urged to go about our daily business as usual—as if nothing had happened. And, indeed, after an emotionally moving appeal on the radio by the prime minister and our beloved old king, Christian X, we did just that. Life went on— Tivoli remained open, the king rode his horse daily through the busy streets in his usual routine, and government, police, and army remained in place with no external evidence of anything unusual having happened, except that we had a lot of armed "guests"—soldiers, airmen, naval and S.S. personnel not to mention tanks—all over the place. It was like a gothic Hans Christian Andersen tale. It was unreal. In retrospect, it seems even odder to realize that Jewish life also went on as usual—Jewish clubs, the Synagogue, the Jewish school, which I attended—all functioned as usual. Well, maybe not exactly as usual. There was an air of tense, ominous anticipation of what might be in store next, an uneasiness that was particularly strong among those in the Jewish community, like my father, who along with many Jews with Eastern European roots, had already experienced pogroms of one kind or another.

During the first years of the German occupation the Danish Resistance movement was rather small, numbering no more than some three thousand in a country of four and a half million. With the help of the Allies and their secret air drops they grew better organized, effective and menacing—having evolved from publishing and distributing illegal newsletters to massive sabotage and bombings of strategic war related factories and rail tracks. This was more than the Germans had bargained for. To them Danes were an affable, apolitical peasant people, and though freedom-loving and strong-headed they were easily handled as long as they were not irritated or provoked too much by display of authority. The very mention of the so-called Jewish problem was an obvious irritant to the Danes—it was none of the Germans' business. It was not to be pursued. At least not right at the start. Yet, the infernal problem of the saboteurs had to be dealt with firmly.

The Germans issued an ultimatum in August 1943. The Danish authorities must see to it that all saboteurs be handed the death penalty. Other encroachments on Danish judicial and governmental autonomy were also at issue. The Government refused to give in to the ultimatum—and all hell broke loose. Christian and Jewish leaders representing all walks of life were arrested as hostages. My father,

Leo Goldberger was a young man when the Germans invaded. "I had just had my Bar Mitzvah in June of 1943. Now perhaps I could do some real resistance work in the underground—not just engage in our childish form of anti-German sentiment: wearing red, white and blue lapel pins, pinching a German soldier in the street, and then running like the devil, or pouring sugar into the gas tank of a German car."

Leo Goldberger's father was the chief cantor at Copenhagen's Great Synagogue.

as a functionary of the Jewish community, was among those to be arrested.

It was the night of August 28, or rather three o'clock in the morning—I was awakened by loud rings and knocks on our front door. It sounded like rifle butts against the door and the heavy metallic footsteps of soldiers. My father quickly came into my brother's and my room and whispered that the Germans were outside and that he would not under any circumstances open the door. For me, this was the most terror-filled moment I had ever experienced. The insistent loud knocks of rifle butts. Fearing that they would break down the door any minute, I implored my father to open it, but he was determined not to. Then, in the nick of time, we heard our upstairs neighbor's voice telling the German soldiers that we—the Goldbergers—were away for the summer, and that three o'clock in the morning was in any case no time to make such a racket! Though they posted a guard outside our apartment building, which we could see through our curtains, we first hid in the bomb shelter accessed through back stairs and then snuck out the back way some 24 hours later with my father in disguise—he had shaven off his Vandyke in order to look less conspicuous. We hastened to the train and headed out of town, my father's face burrowed in a newspaper. It had been his fortieth birthday, August 28th.

We joined the rest of the family—my mother and two younger brothers—who were, indeed, in our rented summer home on the coast near Elsinore. My father had foiled the Germans; he had not become a hostage. But there were even more threatening events to come in the next weeks.

The crisis that had begun in early August reached its crescendo. The Government had stood its ground and finally chose to resign en masse. An entirely new situation in the German-Danish relationship took place on August 29. No more pretense of who ran the show. The country was no longer divided with the government on one side and the resistance movement on the other. It was clearly the Germans who were now in power. The king was under guard at his summer palace. The army was stripped, demobilized. Officers were placed along with the hostages in camps north of Copenhagen. The police and coast guard no longer thought it their duty to carry out anything other than clearly nonpolitical, domestic functions—which excluded apprehending saboteurs or, for that matter, people escaping to Sweden.

By the middle of September, my parents decided that things had cooled down enough for us to return to our apartment in Copenhagen. After all, my brothers and I had to continue school.

Though the idea of escaping to Sweden had rarely surfaced as a viable option before—it was considered almost impossible because of heavy patrols, Danish as well as German—the time was getting close at hand to at least try. Then came the warning—the Germans were planning to round us all up and send us off to a concentration camp, the time was now more than ripe. The warning came near the end of September from a courageous German in the high command's office in Copenhagen—Naval counselor G.F. Duckwitz. It was forwarded to us through Danish intermediaries and announced a few days prior to Rosh Hashanah in the Synagogue. We were urged by Rabbi Melchior to go into hiding and to try and escape to Sweden if possible.

The German plan was to round us up during the night of Rosh Hashanah

Taken in 1942, in the living room in their apartment in Copenhagen, is the Goldberger family (from the left): Leo's brother, Gustave, his father, his brother, Milan, Leo, his mother, and his brother, Erik.

between October 1 and 2, when most Jews presumably would be at home for the high holidays.

Where to hide? Our first night was spent as guests of a wealthy Jewish family who lived in Vedbaek, on the coast some 35 miles away. To our chagrin the family took off for Sweden during the night, without even telling us or their Jewish refugee maid. Apparently my father had been asked by our host whether he wanted to chip in for a boat to take us all to Sweden but had been forced to decline. He simply did not have that kind of money. Near panic but determined to "get tough" and to find a way somehow, my father took a train back to the city; he needed to borrow money, perhaps get an advance on his salary and to see about contacts for passage on a fishing boat. As luck would have it, on the train a woman whom he knew only slightly recognized him and inquired about his obviously agitated facial expression. He confided our plight. Without a moment's hesitation the lady promised to take care of everything. She would meet my father at the main railroad station with all the information about the arrangements within a few hours. It was the least she could do, she said, in return for my father's participation some years back in a benefit concert for her organization—"The Women's League for Peace and Freedom."

After escaping to Sweden, Leo Goldberger became very active in the Jewish scout movement, a group which was organized to fight in the Resistance.

True to her word, she met my father later that day and indicated that all was arranged. The money would be forthcoming from a pastor, Henry Rasmussen (Israel Mission). The sum was a fairly large one—about 25,000 Danish crowns, 5,000 per person, a sum which was more than my father's annual salary. (Though it was ostensibly a loan, I should add that pastor Rasmussen refused repayment after the war.) The next step was to head for a certain address near the coast, less than an hour from Copenhagen. After hurriedly getting some things together from our apartment—a few clothes, some treasured papers and family photos, and, in my case, the newly acquired police flashlight—we were off by taxi to our unknown hosts for the night and our uncertain destiny.

The following night we were standing, huddled in some low bushes along the beach near Dragur, an outskirt of Copenhagen's island of Amager. It was a bitter cold October night. My youngest brother, barely three years old, had been given a sleeping pill to keep him quiet. My brave and stoic little mother was clutching her bag with socks and stockings to be mended which she had taken along for reasons difficult to fathom rationally. We were anxiously and eagerly waiting for the promised light signal. As we were poised to move toward the signal, I could not help but wonder *why* this was all happening. What had we ever done to be in hiding, escaping like criminals? Where would it all end? And why in God's name did the signal not appear? Then finally the lights flashed. We were off! Wading straight into the sea, we walked out some 100 feet through icy water, in water that reached up to my chest. My father carried my two small brothers on his arm. My mother held on to her bag of socks. And I clutched my precious flashlight. My older brother tried valiantly to carry the suitcases but finally had to let them drop in the water. We were hauled aboard the boat, directed in whispers to lie concealed in the cargo area, there to stretch out covered by smelly canvases; in the event the German patrols were to inspect the boat, we would be passed over as fish. There seemed to have been some 20 other Jews aboard. As we proceeded out toward the open sea my father chanted a muted prayer from the Psalms.

A few hours later, bright lights and the pastoral scenery of Skåne along the coast outline of Sweden appeared. Wonderful, peaceful Sweden. A welcoming haven, never to be forgotten, where we remained until our return to Denmark at the end of the war in 1945.

How can I ever forget? How can I ever stop mulling it over, wondering about the whys and wherefores? The Danes were truly fantastic. No doubt about it. Our neighbor upstairs, on the night they came to arrest my father, was great. The lady on the train was an angel. Pastor Rasmussen, a true Christian. The fisherman, although he charged a good penny, was after all diverted from his fishing to the transportation business and needed to make a living. But he *did* risk his life, and was a courageous, yes, a noble soul. And there were thousands of others all across Denmark, helping and caring, tending to us—some 7,200 of us as it turned out. What a magnificent feat! And to think that for the Danes the rescue seemed only natural. Not a big deal, Not something for which special recognition should be given. For them it was the only way. Yet their deed remains in my mind a moral lesson of how we all ought to behave when human beings act cruelly and unjustly and force great suffering on their fellow human beings.

Leo Goldberger after the war when the family returned to Copenhagen.

Leo Goldberger, professor of psychology at New York University, lived in Denmark and was helped by the Danish people to escape to Sweden.

LE CHAMBON

Le Chambon-sur-Lignon.

INTRODUCTION

Le Chambon-sur-Lignon is situated on a high plateau surrounded by rugged mountains in south-central France. It is a place where the winters are very long and very cold. But there, in that little village, during World War II, the climate of the heart was warm, for it was in Le Chambon that people fleeing from the Nazis were welcome and found a place of refuge. Adults as well as children were cared for by people in the village and by peasants from the surrounding countryside. Jewish children taken from internment camps like Gurs and Rivesaltes, were hidden and helped by these good people. There Jewish children went to school and had their lessons together with non-Jewish children from the area. They played tug-of-war and other games. They had a pig named Adolf.

The people of Le Chambon-sur-Lignon not only resisted the Nazis, they resisted the policies of their own country, Vichy France. While there is no single explanation for their actions—perhaps we should leave that to future social scientists—the most important fact for us to know is that they were brought up to understand all the idioms of the language of love. When their hearts spoke to them, they first listened, then they acted.

PIERRE SAUVAGE

MAGDA TROCMÉ

FRANCE

My husband, André Trocmé, was a Protestant minister. During the war, we lived with our four children in the small village of Le Chambon-sur-Lignon in central France. People were content to be there, and we were happy to be able to take care of them, although it was the first time that we lived among peasants. Previously, we had lived in a city, but we appreciated this change, because it is always interesting to get to know different people.

The village of Le Chambon was a Protestant one, with a big church. On Sundays the sermon was something very important, because at that time there were no movies, no special lectures. The sermon was something that everyone wanted to hear. My husband's preaching was different because he was a conscientious objector. The Protestant Church was not happy about it, because at that time conscientious objectors were not admitted as ministers. But the parish wanted a man like my husband, not only because of his ideas about war and peace but on account of his general ideas about truth and justice.

My husband was a very impressive man. He was interesting and genuine, original. He always thought that he had to preach for peace, for better love and under-standing. The parish asked for him because the people wanted him. So later, when the danger came, how could they not back him?

My husband's mother was German and his father French. My father was Italian and my mother was Russian; we were a good combination. We tried to encour-age the parish to be more broad-minded than they perhaps would have been if they had not been living with international people.

We had the opportunity to go to see our families, sometimes in Italy, sometimes in Germany, and we saw what was going on there, especially in Germany. Even before the war, we already knew the truth about what was happening to Jews and others. It was not that we were more clever than the others, but we had more experience and could guess what would happen if the Germans invaded France. Little by little, André tried to prepare the population, preaching to them, preparing them to stand fast. When the dangers came, we were not surprised.

The people in our village knew already what persecutions were because their ancestors were the old Huguenots who, when they accepted the Reformation, were persecuted by the Catholic kings of France. They talked often about their ancestors. Many years went by and they forgot, but when the Germans came, they remembered and were able to understand the persecution of the Jews better perhaps than people in other villages, for they had already had a kind of preparation.

When *la drôle guerre,* the "funny war," was declared in 1939, nothing happened. We knew, of course, that the Germans were coming always nearer to us. We also realized that our government was changing, that Marshal Pétain, who was a very old man, had become the head of the government and that many people believed in him and thought he was like the flag—a symbol—because he was a national hero from World War I. But what many people did not realize was that World War I was very different from World War II.

After the fall of France, André went on preaching as he always did. He spoke against the war. Little by little the Germans, having crossed the border and being in Paris, arrived in our region. The danger was there. They started to persecute the Jews, but we never imagined what would happen to the Jews in France.

Even before the Germans crossed the Vichy line, some Jews managed to get into our part of France, and they tried to come to where we were. It started with the French Jews who often came to our village for the summer. Our peasants were so poor that they took paying guests in the summer. Some of the French Jews were in Le Chambon before the real danger came because they were afraid to stay in the city. They were afraid of the Germans because they knew something about what was happening in Germany. Then the German Jews came. At first, they were paying guests in the hotels and at the farms. Later they became refugees.

Why did they come to us? Because we were in the mountains, because it was a Protestant place, because someone had spoken, perhaps, of a minister who at that time had funny ideas, who was a conscientious objector. You could not know how people knew that they might have a good place in our town. I can tell you what happened in our house, but I cannot tell you what happened in other houses, although I know that little by little there were Jews all over the place.

When the "funny war" started to be a real one, a poor woman came to my house one night, and she asked to come in. She said immediately that she was a German Jew, that she was running away, that she was hiding, that she wanted to have shelter. She thought that at the minister's house she would perhaps find someone who could understand her. And I said, "Come in." And so it started. I

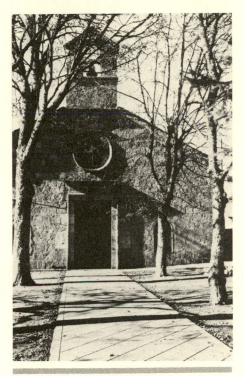

The Protestant temple of Le Chambon-sur-Lignon. "On Sundays the sermon was something very important... something everyone wanted to hear."

André Trocmé was the Protestant minister. "My husband," says Magda Trocmé, "was a very impressive man… He always thought that he had to preach for peace, for better love and understanding. The parish asked for him because the people wanted him. So later, when the danger came, how could they not back him?"

did not know that it would be dangerous. Nobody thought of that.

But all at once, many people were in the village. When you hear that there are nice people who will receive you in their homes in a certain place, and you think you are in danger—and later when you really are in danger—you will do anything to get there. But there was no advertisement. They just came.

Those of us who received the first Jews did what we thought had to be done—nothing more complicated. It was not decided from one day to the next what we would have to do. There were many people in the village who needed help. How could we refuse them? A person doesn't sit down and say I'm going t o do this and this and that. We had no time to think. When a problem came, we had to solve it immediately. Sometimes people ask me, "How did you make a decision?" There was no decision to make. The issue was: Do you think we are all brothers or not? Do you think it is unjust to turn in the Jews or not? Then let us try to help!"

It was not something extraordinary. Now that the years have gone by, perhaps we exaggerate things a little, although I can tell you that things did get complicated later. But in the beginning, when the first Jew came to my house, I just opened the door and took her in without knowing what would happen later. It was even simpler than one might suppose.

In the beginning, we did not realize the danger was so big. Later, we became accustomed to it, but you must remember that the danger was all over. The people who were in the cities had bombs coming down and houses coming in on their heads, and they were killed. Others were dying in the war, in battles. Other people were being persecuted, like those in Germany. It was a general danger, and we did not feel we were in much more danger than the others. And, you see, the danger was not what you might imagine.

You might imagine that the people were fighting with weapons in the middle of the square, that you would have had to run away, that you would have had to go into a little street and hide. The danger was not that kind at all. The danger was in having a government that, little by little, came into the hands of the Germans, with their laws, and the French people were supposed to obey those laws.

The police were no longer "French" police; they were police that acted for the Vichy government that was under the Germans. At that time, we were more afraid of the police and the Vichy government than we were of the Germans, who were not yet really in our country.

We started to disobey in very little ways. For example, in our school it was suggested that we put a picture of Marshal Pétain on the wall. We decided not to do it. It was a small disobedience, but then we started to be more disobedient. In the mornings, to give another example, the flag had to be put up in front of the school and the children were supposed to salute it. We decided not to do it. Ours was a private school, a school founded by the Protestants, not the school of the state. The state school did as the marshal said, but we disobeyed.

Because the director of the public school was one of our friends, he said, "You don't want a flag. I understand. If they want to salute the flag, they can come to my school." At that time, we were just across the street. For a while, some teachers and students went to the flag at the public school. Little by little, it was forgotten and it stopped.

It is true that we had Jewish children in our village. Once when my husband was in Marseilles, he spoke to Burns Chalmers, who was responsible for many of the Quakers' activities on behalf of the inmates of the concentration camps in the south of France. André told him that he wanted to volunteer to go to one of the French camps where there were Jewish children and help take care of them. Chalmers said to him, "But Monsieur Trocmé, we have volunteers for the camps. We have lots of volunteers for the camps. What we do not have is a place, a village, a house, a place to put people who are hiding, people that we can save. We get people out of the camps, but nobody wants them. It is dangerous to take them. Is your village prepared to do such a thing?"

Magda Trocmé in a photograph taken after the war.

My husband came back to the village and he spoke to the council of the church, and they said, "OK, go ahead." Within minutes, they were willing to help. They did not always agree one hundred percent with all that my husband said, but they agreed in general with him, and so they helped.

Yes, there were dangers, but up until then, nothing had happened. More and more we would disobey. We had a habit of doing it. One day, finally, the governor—the prefect of the Department of the Haute-Loire—Monsieur Bach, came and said to my husband, "Now you must give the names of all the Jews that are here." It was at the time that the Jews had to put on the sign, the yellow star.

My husband said, "No, I cannot. First, I do not know their names"—they often changed their names—"and I don't know who they are. And second, these Jews, they are my brothers."

"No," Monsieur Bach said, "they are not your brothers. They are not of your religion. They are not of your country."

"No, you are wrong," André responded. "Here, they are under my protection."

103

The entire Trocmé family in Le Chambon before 1940. In front of André and Magda stand their children: (from the left) Daniel, Jacques, Jean-Pierre, and Nelly.

"You must give me their names," said the prefect, "or who knows? Maybe you will be taken to prison, if you don't tell me who they are."

Immediately I prepared a suitcase. I put into it everything that I thought would be necessary in prison, something warm, a change, and so on. We called that suitcase "the prison suitcase." Then the prefect left, and it was put aside.

Some months later, it was February 13, 1943, around seven o'clock in the evening, two *gendarmes* knocked at the door of the old parsonage in Le Chambon-sur-Lignon. I was cooking and my husband was not home. They asked to see Pastor Trocmé, and I told them that he was at a meeting, and that he was coming back later, but that I could answer all their questions because I knew all about my husband's work. They said that it was something very personal and that they wanted to wait. So I put them in his office, and I went on cooking, doing whatever I had to do, and I forgot about them. When my husband came back, it was about eight o'clock or eight-thirty, he rushed into the house, with his Bible under his arm, with his papers, and went into his office. After awhile he came out and said, "I've been arrested." Why arrested? At that time, nobody even dared to ask why such things happened.

And I said, "Oh my goodness, what about the suitcase?" It was now February and the suitcase was empty, because it had been put together the past August.

And then the *gendarme* said, "What is this suitcase business?" So I told him and he said I could have all the time I needed to prepare André's things, but that no friends or neighbors could be aware of what was happening. These *gendarmes*, you know, were French people, and they were very much worried about doing what they were doing. It was a dirty job, but what could they do? If you are a *gendarme,* you arrest people. There we were, and it was time to eat, so I said to the *gendarmes,* "Sit down and eat."

People now, when they write a book, or when they write a newspaper article, or a magazine article, or when they speak of these things, they say, "Oh, what a wonderful woman. The *gendarmes* came to arrest her husband, and she invited them to sit down and eat with them." It was nothing at all. We always said, "Sit down," when somebody came. Why not say it to the *gendarmes*? And besides, I had to hunt around for the suitcase so that I could pack it. They could just as well sit down and get out of the way.

Before my husband left, you cannot imagine what happened. A young girl, Suzanne Gibert, rang the doorbell. Her father was a church counsellor, and we had been invited to their home because it was her father's birthday. Of course, we had forgotten because of all the excitement. She came, saw the police, ran away, told everyone what was happening in the parsonage, and a few minutes later, the people of the village started a sort of "procession" coming to say good-bye and to bring presents—queer presents, things that we had not seen in years began to appear. A box of sardines, which is nothing now, but at that time a box of sardines was put aside for the worst time, for the future. A candle. We had no candles for light. At the end, we discovered that matches were missing, and the *gendarme* captain gave his own. Someone else brought a piece of soap—we had soap but it was like stone—but somebody brought my husband real soap. And someone brought toilet paper—not a roll, but loose, flat papers. There it was, wonderful toilet paper.

It was only later, when I was able to visit my husband in the camp—it was not a concentration camp, but a Vichy detention camp—that he said to me, "Do you know what was on that paper? With a pencil, very carefully, the person who gave this toilet paper had written on it verses of the Bible, of encouragement, of love and understanding. I had a message, but I don't know from whom."

My husband was a prisoner, and yet someone took the time to write him messages of love and understanding. It was a compensation. People would forget that there was some danger, because they were involved in the work.

I remember once toward the end of June 1943, my husband was not home, and I was called by a girl, Suzanne Heim, early in the morning. She told me that the Gestapo was taking away young people from the student home, "La Maison des Roches." Most of the students there were of military age and foreigners. The Gestapo had gone to the children's home where Daniel Trocmé, my cousin, lived, and had taken him with them to the student home. I went there immediately from my kitchen. I had an apron on, so when I arrived the Gestapo thought I was a maid of the house. They let me in, and I sat in the kitchen. I tried to go into the dining room where all the Jewish students were in a line. My cousin Daniel who was responsible for the students was with them. The Gestapo screamed at me and kicked me out, but they let me go into the kitchen, which meant that they thought I was a maid, that I was someone belonging to the house. After a while I had to go to the village.

When I returned, my young son Jean-Pierre, who was 13, came to be with me for the moment when the students were taken, because he did not want me to be alone. I saw all those boys passing to go into a little room where there was a man with a booklet with many names. He was interrogating them, interviewing them one by one. Most of those who went through had a little bit of paper and said to me, "Send this to my mother. Here's the address of my father. This is for my fiancée. I have some money in my room." They did not know that all the rooms had already been searched and that there was no longer any money, no jewels in the rooms. But it did not matter. We would help them anyhow if possible. My son was so upset when he saw those Gestapo beating those Jews as they were in line coming down the stairs, going into the trucks. They were beating some of those young boys and screaming, *"Schweine Juden! Schweine Juden!"*

We saw all those young people get into the trucks, and my cousin Daniel said to me, "Do not worry. Tell my parents that I was very happy here. It was the best time of my life. Tell them that I like traveling, that I go with my friends."

For many refugees, the "poetic gate" of the presbytery was the real entrance into the village of refuge. To the left of the door is the ancient coat of arms of the village.

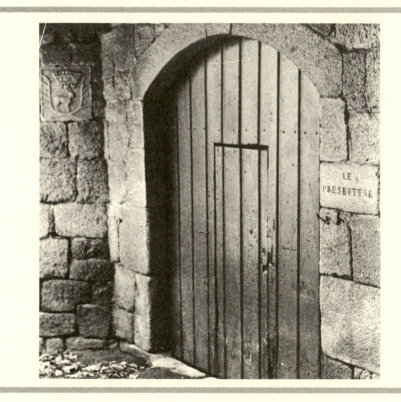

When they left, my son was green, I would say, like a sick boy. And he said, "Mother, I am going to get revenge later. Such things cannot happen again. I am going to do something when I am grown up." And I said to him, "But you know what your father says: 'If you do such a thing, someone else is going to take revenge against you. And that is why we are never finished. We go on and on and on. We must forgive, we must forget, we must do better.'" He was silent, and we left. And Daniel never came back.

During the war things were very difficult. When my husband after a few weeks did return safely from the Vichy camp, we continued our work taking care of people. After the war, I traveled in America for the Fellowship of Reconciliation. I spoke English at that time much better. I was asked lots of times to speak about these things, to say what the lesson was that we must learn from all this.

The lesson is very simple, I think. The first thing is that we must not think that we were the only ones who helped during those times. Little by little, now that we speak of these things, we realize that other people did lots of things too. Also, we must not be afraid to be discussed in books or in articles and reviews, because it may help people in the future to try to do something, even if it is dangerous. Perhaps there is also a message for young people and for children, a message of hope, of love, of understanding, a message that could give them the courage to go against all that they believe is wrong, all that they believe is unjust.

Maybe later on in their lives, young people will be able to go through experiences of this kind—seeing people murdered, killed, or accused improperly; racial problems; the problem of the elimination of people, of destroying perhaps not their bodies but their energy, their existence. They will be able to think that there always have been some people in the world who tried—who will try—to give hope, to give love, to give help to those who are in need, whatever the need is.

It is important, too, to know that we were a bunch of people together. This is not a handicap, but a help. If you have to fight it alone, it is more difficult. But we had the support of people we knew, of people who understood without knowing precisely all that they were doing or would be called to do. None of us thought that we were heroes. We were just people trying to do our best.

When people read this story, I want them to know that I tried to open my door. I tried to tell people, "Come in, come in." In the end, I would like to say to people, "Remember that in your life there will be lots of circumstances that will need a kind of courage, a kind of decision of your own, not about other people but about yourself." I would not say more.

Magda Trocmé, who with her daughter, Nelly Trocmé-Hewett, is in the movie, "The Courage to Care," lives in Paris, France. During the German occupation of France, she and her husband, Pastor André Trocmé, helped Jews hide in and around the village of Le Chambon. Madame Trocmé and her husband have been honored by Yad Vashem.

Major
Julius
Schmahling

PHILIP HALLIE

I want to tell you about a certain German army officer who, while being dutiful, and even efficient, in Hitler's military managed to save the lives of many people in the mountains of southern France. He was a good man who was part of an evil cause, and so his story is paradoxical at its very center. First, I want to give you a·context in which you can understand this paradoxical man.

After having spent a large part of my adult life studying the evil perpetuated by the German nation between 1933 and 1945, I found it necessary for my emotional well-being to seek out what goodness, what hope I could salvage from the story of those years. Happily, I found the village of Le Chambon, a tiny village in the Cévennes Mountains of southeastern France that saved thousands of children from the gas chambers and the deep pits. The goodness of the people of Le Chambon did not reside only in saving those young lives; it resided also in the fact that the more than three thousand people in that village did not hate or kill anyone, even the children-killers. Ethics is the celebration of life, and throughout the years from 1940 to 1945, when the Germans occupied France, they celebrated life by both helping the defenseless and not hating or hurting their victimizers. Unlike soldiers or guerilla fighters they were no person's enemies. They were morally pure, uncompromising in their efficacious caring.

But when I finished finding and writing out their story in my book, *Lest Innocent Blood Be Shed* (Harper and Row, 1979), I found myself with two puzzles. The first was: How did they manage to protect the bitterest enemies of the Germans—Jews—for four long years without being utterly smashed? How did that little train manage to keep coming in, afternoon after afternoon, with refugees aboard, filling up that "nest of Jews in Huguenot country," as Le Chambon was called throughout the region, without the Germans and their French collaborators massacring them all?

The second puzzle was: Who was *"Le major,"* the major I had heard so much about? Many times when I was living in the village, and when I was interviewing villagers now living elsewhere, I would mention my puzzle about the survival of this village packed with Hitler's worst enemies. And many times I got the simple answer, *"Ah! C'était le major."* "It was the major." When I pursued the question, all I learned was that he was a German named Julius Schmahling, who had a position of responsibility in the government of the region during the last two years of the occupation of France.

The first details I learned about him were in the autobiographical notes of the leader of Le Chambon, Pastor André Trocmé. These notes simply stated that he saved the lives of many people in the Haute-Loire, of which he was occupation governor in 1943, until he was replaced by an ardent Nazi, Colonel Metger. Apparently the major was considered to be too soft and too old—he was about sixty years old then—to administer this dangerous and sensitive region of France, and he was replaced by a tough career officer fresh from the brutal war in Russia. But Schmahling stayed on as second-in-command until the end of the war in France in August 1944.

But these facts did not clear up my puzzles. They did not tell me if, and if, how, he saved the lives of so many people in the region and protected the rescue machine of Le Chambon from his fellow Germans.

The solutions to my puzzles were becoming very important to me. After writing a book about this morally pure group of people, the people of Le Chambon, I found myself depressed. I felt so small, so impure compared to them. I began to feel that my book about them was not a concrete story that had meaning for me and people like me—it was more of a parable, or an allegory about ideal creatures, who happened to have been real. I even found myself resenting the pure-hearted *Chambonnais*—they had not killed, and I had. They hadn't tried to stop Hitler's armies, and I had, as a combat soldier in Europe during the last year of the war. They were too good for *me* to understand, because in the war, and at other times, I had compromised with my profound revulsion against hating and harming my fellow human beings. I had found myself thinking one day, "Oh yes, these *Chambonnais* were good people, but people like me, haters and killers, *stopped* Hitler, kept him from spreading his art of cruelty and murder across the face of our earth."

And here, in the major, I found a man like us. He did some good, just as I have done some good, but he was deeply implicated, deeply compromised by doing harm. He was closer to me, this German I might have killed without a qualm during the war, than those almost angelic Frenchmen and Frenchwomen! It occurred to me that if I could understand why I admired this man in spite of his duty to Hitler's Third Reich, I might learn something about admiring—or at least being friends with other maculate beings, like my family, and like myself. I might

110

learn something about the goodness I see around me, whenever I *look* and *see*, though it might be a tainted goodness.

I lived with his children in Germany. (They are middle-aged like me, and his son was a German soldier in battles in which I fought opposite him.) The more I found out about him and the more I learned from talking to my various friends in the Resistance in the Haute-Loire, the more clearly I saw how deeply tainted he was. One of the reasons he could protect the village, and others in the region, was that he was a friend of the dreaded Armed-S.S. general, Josef ("Sepp") Dietrich. Dietrich was one of the original henchmen of Adolf Hitler in the streets and beer halls of Munich, and he had participated in the "Night of the Long Knives" in 1934. On that night he helped wipe out the S.A. (the Stormtroopers) leadership. He was rightly called "the learned butcher."

They first met in the north of France, when Schmahling was criticizing the arrogant and cruel behavior of Dietrich's S.S. men. Both of them were plainspoken Bavarians who had the same outgoing, sensual temperaments, and they also shared a great respect for inferiors who could be critical without being disloyal. They both loved food and drink, and loved to talk on the telephone.

And on the telephone they kept their friendship alive after Schmahling left his post in the north of France in order to take over the Haute-Loire in the south. I have no record of those telephone conversations, but French people who worked in Schmahling's office in France, and Schmahling's children have convinced me that these telephone conversations—and one visit between Dietrich and Schmahling in the south—had much to do with Schmahling's power to protect the region from Klaus Barbie and other Gestapo chiefs in the south. The Armed S.S. and the Gestapo were at the peak of the Nazi power structure, and they shared not only theories and practices but personnel with each other. A word from Dietrich on the telephone could, and I am convinced, did prevent Gestapo raids in the Haute-Loire.

But the force that helped Schmahling protect people in the Haute-Loire, and people in Le Chambon in particular, also compromised Schmahling deeply. Schmahling was supping with the Devil, and he had to be careful not to offend one of the most powerful leaders of the Third Reich.

Still, tainted as he was, how could he save "many people in the region," as Pastor André Trocmé put it? At first I thought that Schmahling might be a deeply religious man practising Christian love quietly. Like most Bavarians he was a Catholic. But it turns out that he was totally nonreligious. When he was in his teens he scandalized and pained his mother, who begged him to go to church.

Julius Schmahling in Munich, Germany, 1939.

He refused to go—except to admire the architecture. When a friend would meet him in the street and would say, "I haven't seen you in church, Julius," he would usually answer, "You see me better out here. It's lighter outside."

He was a high school teacher in southern Germany before and after the war, and one would think that as a teacher of history and literature he would be articulate about what he believed; but when any of his students or colleagues would ask him what he meant by calling somebody "good" or "wicked" instead of presenting a neat theory of ethics he would almost always utter one little sentence, "What's right is obvious, obvious." As a student of philosophy, I found it impossible to find any principles in his speech or in his behavior.

Julius Schmahling in Le Puy (Haute Loire), France, 1943.

All I found was what he once described as "my hot-blooded passion." He loved the present, and was full of compassion for those who came to him for help. He had no plans or goals—only passionate and compassionate reactions to his own and to other people's present needs. He was baroque, unruly, exuberant, not classical or restrained or lucid. As a civilian and as a reserve officer he was the exact opposite of the "orders-are-orders" personality. He lived spontaneously. For instance, when his friends were driving him somewhere he would urge them to run the stop signs and run the red traffic lights if he wanted to be there *now*. Duty-oriented types would follow orders from above—not he. He was not a man who *had things to do;* he was a man who *had to do things* out of the boiling wellspring of his immense physical and mental health.

Instead of going into the depths of his soul, or claiming to do so, let me tell you two stories about him. He was a young teacher in northern Bavaria when one day he came into his wooden classroom to give his students a lesson on lions. He had prepared a dramatic lesson on the king of beasts, and full of it, and of himself, he walked into the classroom. As he spoke the first words, "The lions," he noticed a little boy in the back of the room who had been sitting dumbly on his wooden bench during the whole term. The boy was waving his hand in the air trying to catch his teacher's eye. The young teacher kept talking about the great beasts. In a few moments the boy jumped off his bench and called out "Herr Professor, Herr—" Schmahling looked at him in anger—he could not believe that this little dunce was going to interrupt his discourse on lions. Then the boy did something that really amazed the teacher. He called out, without permission, "Yesterday, yes, yesterday I saw a rabbit! Yesterday I really saw a rabbit!"

Before the words were all out, Schmahling yelled out, "Sit down, you little jackass." The boy sat down, and never said a word for the rest of the year.

In his old age, Schmahling looked back at that moment as the most decisive one in his whole life. Then, while he was crushing the boy with all the power of German pedagogical authoritarianism, he was destroying something in himself in the very act of destroying the moment of sunlight in that little boy's life. When the class was over he vowed to himself that he would never do such a thing again to a human being. Teaching and living for him, he vowed, would from that moment forward involve making room for each of his students and each of the people he knew outside of the classroom to speak about the rabbits they had seen.

Julius Schmahling with other German officers, in Le Puy (Haute Loire), France, 1943.

And he kept his vow. It was as simple as that—and as infinitely complex as keeping such a vow during the German occupation of France. If he had had a complicated ideology or theory he might well have been recognized as a *Gegner*, an enemy of the Third Reich, and might well have been smashed. As it was, he was no ideological threat to the Nazis around him. This was why Dietrich could like him—because he was simply likable, and likably simple.

In his nonreligious, nonprincipled way he carved out an ethical space for caring in his classrooms and in his duties as the military governor of the Haute-Loire in 1943 and 1944. He was no hero, no declared enemy of Nazism or of any other "ism"—seen from a distance he was just one dutiful member of the Nazi war machine. But seen up close, and seen from the point of view of the hundreds, possibly thousands, of people he protected from the Gestapo and from his own vicious auxiliary troops in the Haute-Loire, he was a good man. He compromised with evil, and helped defenseless people as much as he could. He did not try to save everybody, the way German heroes like Dietrich Bonhoeffer and Kurt Gerstein did—he tried only to save a few people, and he succeeded in that limited task. But seen from the distant point of view of history he was an obedient part of the paw of the monster that was Nazism. He was a good man in an evil cause.

In his last days in the Haute-Loire, after the Germans had been defeated in France, he was called in for a *"séance"* before the local Resistance chiefs. A *séance* was an informal court hearing, usually preparatory for a full court hearing, or, in some cases, for summary execution. As a German he was the target of all the frustrations and angers the French felt after four years of murderously cruel and humiliating occupation. There had been a massacre of Germans just a few miles to the north, and to the east 50 Germans were being killed and dumped into a great well.

At this time, on August 20, 1944, the door of the room in the Haute-Loire was opened, and in walked the former Commandant of one of the most dangerous regions in occupied France. Julius Schmahling at the age of 60 was a small, rotund man, with a balding, egg-shaped head. As he rolled down the aisle with his sturdy body and in his slightly worn, green-gray, *Wehrmacht* officer's uniform, he was not a figure of distinction, and he seemed an easy target for all the hatred the French were feeling then against the Germans.

But when he got halfway down the aisle everybody in the room, including the toughest chiefs of the Haute-Loire Resistance, stood up and turned to him. As he walked up the aisle, people whispered to him, "Major, do you need more food in jail? Do you need writing materials or books?" As he walked, he smiled, and shook his head gently.

When he came up to the head of the tribunal, the tough old French Resistance chief who was chairman of the *séance* bowed to him (for he had stood up with all of the others) and made a little speech of gratitude to him on the part of all of the Frenchmen in the Haute-Loire.

Later, in his diary, Schmahling described the meeting as *"fast peinlich,"* almost painful: he was glad for their praise and their affection, but didn't they realize decency is the normal thing to do? Didn't they realize that decency needs no rewards, no recognition, that it is done out of the heart, now, immediately, just in order to satisfy the heart now?

This was Major Julius Schmahling, who in the midst of battle made room for thoughts and acts of love unconsoled, unsupported by religion or by ethical or political principles. In studying him and in learning to admire him, I have learned much about respecting myself and others in a maculate world. I have learned that ethics is not simply a matter of good and evil, true north and true south. It is a matter of mixtures, like most of the other points on the compass, and like the lives of most of us. We are not all called upon to be perfect, but we can make a little, real difference in a mainly cold and indifferent world. We can celebrate human life in a local, intimate celebration, even with the coldness not far away.

Philip Hallie, Griffin Professor of philosophy and humanities at Wesleyan University, is the author of many works, including Lest Innocent Blood be Shed, *(Harper and Row, 1979) a book about Le Chambon.*

Hans Solomon
Hanne Liebmann
Rudy Appel

THREE SURVIVORS

Hans Solomon: I arrived in Le Chambon-sur-Lignon on Friday, the 13th, which was, thank God, a golden Friday instead of a black Friday. We were roughly 40 students, mixed—Jews and non-Jews. Half were non-Jewish boys and the other half were Jewish boys liberated from concentration camps, mostly the Camp de Rivesaltes and the Camp de Gurs. These camps were not extermination camps like Auschwitz and Buchenwald, but the conditions were extremely bad. Starvation was the main thing that killed people, and it was very common.

At first, in Le Chambon, we Jewish boys kept to ourselves. We remained quite separate from the gentile boys, some of whom were liberated in the same way we were. Within two weeks, however, after Pastor Trocmé had talked to us and we all knew that we were free at last and could talk as we wanted, we began to relax.

It got worse in August 1942, when part of the Gestapo found out that Jews were being hidden in the Maison des Roches in Le Chambon. What happened was that at night all the Jewish boys were taken in by farmers in the neighborhood. We slept in the barns and in the stables and in the morning we would walk back to the Maison des Roches, where we went to school.

We had a way of knowing if it was safe or not to return to school in the morning. One gentile boy was in charge. If the coast was clear, he would open the shutters on the window of his room; if the Gestapo were in the house, he would not open the shutters. It was very important. One morning we walked toward the Maison des Roches, and we saw that the shutters were closed. Immediately, we went back to our farmers, where they again took us in and we stayed overnight.

Of course, we could not forget that our parents, our aunts and uncles were still in concentration camps, but we younger people had a will to live. It was given to us by the people of Le Chambon and by an American man, Tracy Strong, who as vice president of the European Student Fund was partly instrumental in getting Jewish boys liberated from the Rivesaltes detention camp to Le Chambon.

Hanne Liebmann: Originally, there were seven of us young people who came from the concentration camp in Gurs. In the camp, we were asked whether we would like to leave and go to a French village. We were not given a lot of information, other than that there were people who wanted to take youngsters out of the camp, that they wanted to help us, that there was a Protestant pastor involved, and that the community at large supported him in his effort. I said, "Yes, I want to leave," and that was that.

We came to Le Chambon, the seven of us, and we were received very wonderfully. Of course, to us, even a warm meal, a complete meal, was a tremendous

La Maison des Roches where young Jewish students stayed during the war.

thing. We were placed in a home where there were about 20 or 25 boys and girls from outside of France, some French Jewish children, and some non-Jewish children—all sorts of children. We really found a haven there.

Then, in 1942, things became more dangerous, and we had to be hidden. We were taken to farms, and the farmers took us without a question. They were happy to have us, and they shared their bread with us, though there was very

118

little of that. I can say that I think my faith in humankind—perhaps this is true for all of us—was really reestablished by those gentle people.

Rudy Appel: My experience was that there was no pressure at all for Jewish children to become Christian. And I think, undoubtedly, that the temptation must have been great for them to try to influence us, to encourage us to convert. But, in fact, with the help of Pastor Trocmé, we held our own religious services on the Jewish Holy Days, either in the Protestant Temple of Le Chambon or in the school. I have not heard of anyone who was under pressure at any time to become a Christian.

The Christians in Le Chambon had a fundamentalist belief that the Jewish people, or the Jewish religion, was the basis of their own religion, and, therefore, that the people who were Jews—believers of that ancient faith—had to be protected, that to protect them was to do the work of God. I sensed this throughout my stay in Le Chambon, even though they might not have been able to put this basic belief into words themselves, they felt it in their souls. In fact, I think this fundamentalist belief is alive even today in le Chambon.

Hans Solomon, Hanne Liebmann, and Rudy Appel, all Jewish survivors sheltered in Le Chambon, now live in the United States.

REFLECTIONS

Why Were
There
So Few?

ELIE WIESEL

I am going to tell you a story. It happened in May 1944, somewhere in Eastern Europe. A ghetto entered the last phase of its brief, convulsive existence. Transports. Deportation. Destination unknown. I remember the unique destiny of that evening, the quietness that hung over the ghetto in secret turmoil, the 30 to 40 neighbors gathering in our courtyard, and their whispers, "Where are we going? For what purpose?"

We were the last living Jews in occupied Europe, and we had never heard of Treblinka and Birkenau, but we felt the threat. Somebody was knocking at the window facing the other side of the ghetto. Who could that be? By the time we managed to open the window, the person had vanished. Later, an eternity later, my father and I would recall that incident. My father was convinced that a gentile friend had tried to warn us—and perhaps, to save us from our collective appointment with death at Auschwitz.

Why did that unknown person choose to stand between a Jewish family and its enemy. What motivated him or her, what made him or her different from so many others?

What is memory if not an attempt to increase humankind's sensitivity by enlarging the scope of its awareness? If I had to choose between feeling the burning of scars or not feeling at all, I would choose the former. Numbness was a danger then, and it still is today. Your encounters in this book may bring you some joy—and much sadness. It is important to feel them both.

When we look at all those collaborators, accomplices, and passive onlookers, our memory is invaded by sadness. Treblinka was so near Warsaw, Maidanek so near Lublin, and Babi-Yar near Kiev—no, Babi-Yar is *in* Kiev; it *is* Kiev. Is it possible that the inhabitants of Kiev didn't know? They saw the long processions of Jews going to the ravine; they heard the shooting. How is it that they did not open their doors for a child here, a grandfather there?

But, on the other hand, there were some men and women who, in many places, did opt for humanity. Surrounded by terror, oppressed by absolute evil, they had the courage to care about their fellow human beings. Isn't that a reason for us to feel comforted and, indeed, uplifted? These individuals *did* save a Jewish woman, a Jewish family. Where did they find the courage to care? They were not protected by visible or invisible armies, nor did many of them belong to organized clandestine movements. They were alone—as the victims themselves were alone—and so the question we must confront is what made them so special, so human, so different?

Why Denmark? Why Bulgaria? Why are most rescuers anonymous people who just happen to belong to that noble category of human beings who act simply because of their commitment to humanity? You will find among them few high-ranking officers, renowned writers, or influential politicians, and my question to you is, Why? What happened to the well-educated liberals and humanists, those who loudly proclaim how much they care for every victim, how tirelessly they will fight against every injustice, and how deeply they will get involved in every battle for decency and dignity. Why did *they* choose to remain insensitive to the plight, the tragedy, the murder of Jewish men and women and children? Was it a choice? If not, what was it?

These are difficult and disturbing questions and they lead inevitably to others. Why was the tragedy of the Jews treated as a low-ranking priority in so many quarters? Why did the brave German officers who attempted to assassinate Hitler on July 20, 1944, totally neglect the moral element and forget to mention that their plan had been motivated by moral imperatives linked to Germany's Final Solution? Why did the French police collaborate with Eichmann's emissaries in rounding up French Jews in 1942?

If the rescuers of the Jews justify our faith in humankind, they must also—on another level—justify our suspicion of society; for each Oskar Schindler, how many accomplices were there? For each Raoul Wallenberg, how many black-mailers, how many *schmalzowniks*? When we allow ourselves to become captivated by the melancholy beauty of the rescuers' gestures, let us also never forget the savage scenery surrounding them.

Raoul Wallenberg and Charles Lutz were helped by brave young Zionists in Budapest; clandestine groups were active in many cities, in many countries, helping Jews to steal across borders to relative safety and then to the land of Israel—a country which, since the war, has taught all the others a lesson: that it is possible to save whole communities from persecution and threat.

Remember that it was easy to save human lives. One did not need to be heroic or crazy to feel pity for an abandoned child. It was enough to open a door, to throw a piece of bread, a shirt, a coin—it was enough to feel compassion. It would have been enough for the U.S. Department of State to send more visas. In those times one climbed to the summit of humanity simply by remaining human.

The principle that governs the biblical vision of society is, "Thou shall not stand idly by when your fellow man is hurting, suffering, or being victimized." It is because that injunction was ignored or violated that the catastrophe involving such multitudes occurred. The victims perished not only because of the killers, but also because of the apathy of the bystanders. Those who perished were victims of Nazism and of society—though to different degrees. What astonished us after the torment, after the tempest, was not that so many killers killed so many victims, but that so few cared about us at all.

The Holocaust was made possible because of the enemy's successful efforts to divide humankind into innumerable opposing categories. The old were pitted against the young, the rich against the poor, nationals against strangers, friend against friend—and all against the Jews. The memory of the Holocaust therefore is meant to bring us all together. If it divides those who study its meaning, then we shall continue to bear its weight of malediction; but if we resist divisiveness and realize that though a unique Jewish tragedy, it had universal implications, we may see in memory a haven and refuge for all our children.

Elie Wiesel, author, teacher, and human rights activist, is the Andrew Mellon Professor in the Humanities at Boston University. He is the Chairman of the United States Holocaust Memorial Council.

"What astonished us after the torment, after the tempest, was not that so many killers killed so many victims, but that so few cared about us at all."

Examples
of
Heroism

MOSHE
BEJSKI

There is a Talmudic saying that whoever saves one life, it is as if he saved the entire world. These are the words engraved on the medal that Yad Vashem presents to those found deserving of the title, "Righteous Among the Nations." For 30 years we at Yad Vashem have been searching out these selfless people who, on their own initiative and following the dictates of their consciences, came to the aid of their fellow human beings. By their actions they saved not only the tormented Jews whom they took under their protection, but also the honor of all humankind. Those noble individuals living in occupied Europe who refused to countenance the fate that the Nazis had pronounced upon the Jews overrode their fears about the personal risk involved and, without anticipation of remuneration or personal gain, put their lives on the line to save others.

The truth is that it is not easy to find them all. They acted in secrecy, and even after the war was over, some of them chose to remain anonymous. In a number of instances the Jews they saved perished later in the war, leaving no one to recount the story of the things they did. There are other cases in which the rescuers perished together with the Jews they were hiding when their deeds were discovered.

After carefully examining the evidence for every individual case brought to our attention, we on Yad Vashem's Committee for the Designation of the Righteous Among the Nations have found so far about 4,700 individuals who, in the spirit of the Martyrs' and Heroes' Remembrance Law (1953), are worthy of the title "Righteous Among the Nations." We have been able to draw two principal conclusions from the cases we have examined.

First, the ways in which people from various parts of the population helped or saved others were truly remarkable and widely varied, whether it was by sharing a meager portion of food—like the 16-year-old girl who, day after day, brought a slice of bread to the Jewish woman prisoner with whom she worked in a weapons factory—or by supplying forged papers that would enable a Jew to pass as a non-Jew, and thereby be exempted from the transport to Auschwitz and

Treblinka. Some benefactors went so far as to build hiding places and bunkers in their apartments and places of business—as did the people who hid Anne Frank and her family—and kept a Jewish family for weeks, months, even years—thereby placing themselves and their own families in constant peril.

Many cases have come to our attention. Behind every one of them is an extraordinary tale of unsung valor. One of these is the story of an impoverished farmer who lived on the edge of a forest in which a unit of Jewish partisans was hiding. He served as their contact with the outside world and their sole source of food. When an informer made this action known to the S.S., the farmer was ordered to lead them to the forest hideout. He refused and was subsequently shot and killed in front of his wife. Threatened with a similar fate if she did not reveal the partisans' hiding place, she, too, refused—and was similarly murdered. It is difficult to appreciate fully the heroism of this act of honor, for its significance lay not only in the rescue of a unit of partisans, but in the supreme humanity of the act.

Jewish legend has it that the world reposes upon 36 Just Men, the *Lamed Vov,* who are indistinguishable from simple mortals and whose identity is never revealed. During the Holocaust, they had helpers. Alongside acts of unprecedented cruelty were the deeds of a few thousand such righteous souls who for their time salvaged the honor of all humankind. The regrettable thing is that there were only a few thousand, while millions of courageous men and women were needed to save the millions of Jews whom the Germans were determined to destroy. Unfortunately, when the time came, millions were not to be found.

Second, from the thousands of files we have handled at Yad Vashem, we have learned that it was possible to aid and to rescue Jews in every known circumstance—even within the death camps themselves. In Auschwitz, for example, there was an extraordinary, selfless physician, Dr. Adelaide Hautval, who was sent to the camp because she had protested so adamantly to the Gestapo in France about their cruel treatment of the Jews.

Dr. Hautval found herself in the famous experimental Block 10, and later in the death factory in Birkenau. Not only did she refuse to cooperate with the infamous Dr. Mengele and Drs. Agrad and Wirths in their experiments on Jewish women, but she cared for the Jewish prisoners with her loving hands. When an epidemic of typhoid broke out and all the patients would probably have been sent to the gas chambers, Dr. Hautval hid them in bunks and nursed them with maternal devotion. She truly earned for herself the sobriquets "The White Angel" and "The Saint." In 1984, I visited Dr. Hautval in France, and throughout the years of my association with her—ever since she was honored as one of the "Righteous Among the Nations"—I have repeatedly concluded that she is to be counted among the 36 Just for whom the world is sustained.

There was no limit to the ways in which it was possible to help and save people, nor was there any end to the forms of initiative taken by the stouthearted men and women of conscience who are credited with saving one or many souls. Each acted according to the circumstances, the extent of his or her ability, and the risk he or she was prepared to take.

Raoul Wallenberg's work in saving 30 thousand Jews in Budapest is well known. He took on the special mission of extending aid to the Jews of Hungary at the very time when transports were leaving Budapest for Auschwitz every day—ten thousand deportees a day. On his own initiative, when he reached Budapest, he began to print up Swedish certificates of protection and distributed them among the Jews slated for deportation. When he saw that the authorities were honoring these documents, he went on to establish the so-called international ghetto. At a certain stage, this colony absorbed 33 thousand people who were cared for and protected from deportation to Auschwitz.

Recently, I met with a close aide of Wallenberg's from that period, Per Anger of Sweden, and heard additional details about their work, which included drawing people out of the death marches that were headed toward the Austrian border. Wallenberg drove up to the columns with truckloads of food and medical supplies, distributing them among the marchers to ease their suffering, and he continued to release from the transport any person he could possibly liberate on the basis of any slip of paper imaginable. This truly dazzling display of resourcefulness was the work of a single man. He saved tens of thousands of Jews by exploiting every opportunity to aid, ease, and rescue. Arrested by the Soviets on the day they entered Budapest, he never returned from the Soviet Union. The Kremlin's protestations that he succumbed to a heart attack in Lubyanka prison have been shown to be false, and we may never know the real truth about this episode.

At a certain stage the Swiss, Spanish, and Portuguese embassies took a number of Hungarian Jews under their protection. But for the most part, the Righteous Gentiles acted as individuals, sometimes for purely humanitarian reasons, sometimes from profound religious conviction. In some places, such as Norway and Holland, they operated in the framework of the anti-Nazi underground.

It was not easy to swim against the current in an atmosphere of fear and hostility—especially in light of the enormous risk that a person and his family took in aiding a Jew. During this era of darkness, in the climate of incitement against the Jews and widespread inhumanity, the actions of those isolated individuals are all the more outstanding.

Unfortunately, anyone who extended a hand to aid a Jew could not expect any help, either from the outside world or from his immediate environment. To the contrary, from the viewpoint of the Nazi regime, if such a deed became known, the rescuer stood to suffer the same fate as the Jew who had been taken under his protection.

These fine, principled people did not even receive any consideration from their own countrymen. Take, for example, the case of the Swiss police officer Paul Grueninger. After the annexation of Austria, he turned a blind eye to the passage of a certain number of persecuted refugees over the Swiss border—which the authorities had closed. Tried and convicted of a dereliction of his formal duty for this humanitarian act, he was dismissed from his position and denied his pension. It took 30 years for him to get his due. It was only after he was recognized by Yad Vashem as one of the "Righteous Among the Nations" that a public outcry arose against the injustice done to him, and he was rehabilitated.

Similarly, the Portuguese minister in Bordeaux found that he could not follow his government's orders forbidding entry to Jewish refugees who, fleeing the Nazis, had reached southern France in 1940. Thousands of such refugees were crowding the streets of the city, and Aristides de Souza Mendes could not be on the side of terror. Following his conscience, absolutely contrary to orders, he granted entry visas to homeless and defenseless Jews and paid for his humanity with his position and his career. Stripped of all his prerogatives by the Portuguese government, he remained faithful to his principles and sense of humanity to the day he died, in exile, here in the United States.

Yad Vashem has recently completed a thorough study of the quite extraordinary case in which the whole populace of a village acted as rescuers. In fact, we have seen only one such case for the entire period—that of the Dutch village of Niuvelande. (I have not forgotten the French village of Le Chambon, but it is somewhat different.)

In 1942-43 the residents of Niuvelande decided that every household would take and hide one Jewish family or, at least, an individual Jew. And that is precisely what they did. It was only in such a collective action that the risk was diminished. No one feared being informed upon by his neighbor, because all were equally implicated in the "crime" of concealing a Jew.

In speaking of collective action, one must mention the rescue of about 7,200 Jews of Denmark, who were transferred to Sweden in a special operation mounted by the Danish people. The transfer was accomplished in small boats, over three nights, at a time when the port of Copenhagen was already teeming with boats sent by the Nazis to carry the Jews of Denmark to their death. Denmark is the only country in occupied Europe that succeeded, through a common effort, in saving—virtually at the eleventh hour—almost all of its Jews. It is hardly necessary to explain that this was possible only because of the willingness of so many who were willing to lend a hand in the rescue venture. It is a sign of the greatness of the Danish people and will never be forgotten, for it shows what might have been done throughout Europe, had a similar readiness to act been in evidence in other countries.

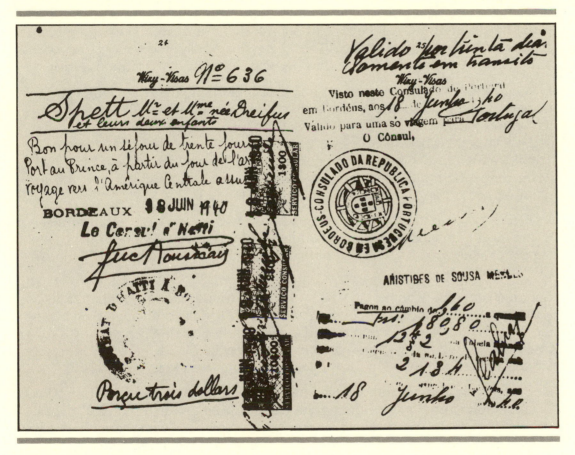

Transit visa issued contrary to his government's wishes by Aristides de Sousa Mendes, Portuguese Consul in Bordeaux, France, June 18, 1940. (His signature is directly adjacent to the consular stamp.) Like thousands of others he signed, this visa allowed the Spett family to escape from France. Michael Spett, then five years old, came later with his family to New York City. He now is president of the printing firm, re-established by his father, which designed and manufactured this book.

In referring to the rescue of Danish Jewry, it is important to mention the name of another Righteous Gentile, a German who contributed enormously to the success of the Danish rescue operation: the naval attaché at the German Embassy in Copenhagen, Georg Ferdinand Duckwitz.

Aware of what might befall the Jews of Denmark, Duckwitz did not hesitate. When the time came for their deportation in 1943, he warned Danish Resistance leaders about why the German boats were coming into port and what was about to take place. The disclosure of this plan by Duckwitz—whose information was known to be both solid and reliable—convinced the Jews and the Danish people of the immediate danger. They all went into frantic action to carry out the massive and perilous rescue operation that is credited with saving almost all the Jews of Denmark.

For a number of years now, Yad Vashem has been preparing a lexicon of all those who have been recognized as "Righteous Among the Nations," and the day is not far off when we will be able to publish this commemoration of the rescue actions of these men and women. The "Righteous Among the Nations" deserve to have their deeds known by all and to become a part of our common legacy.

I do not know whether anyone who has not undergone the harrowing experiences of being pursued to death by the Nazi regime can fully appreciate the terror and torment known by the Jews of occupied Europe. For more than five and a half years, when all doors were closed and all roads led to Auschwitz, Treblinka, Belzec, Sobibor, and other camps, I lived with these feelings. I shall never forget the humiliation, the hostility fairly crackling all around me, the sensation of being trapped with no hand extended in aid.

In 1942 I was able to escape the camp where I was imprisoned, and returned to my parents' village in Poland. When the final action was conducted to deport the surviving Jews for extermination in the Belzec death camp, I eluded the Germans.

But then came the searches, in which every Jew found hiding was summarily shot. I managed to flee from the S.S., and at night I walked through the snow to the house of a Polish friend in a nearby village. I hoped to stay there for a day or two, until the men of the *Sonderkommando* (Special Details in the death camps) left the vicinity and the hunt for the Jews in hiding was over.

He was a school friend with whom I had studied for seven years. All I asked was to take refuge in the pigpen during the daylight hours, so that the next night I could move on. But he wouldn't let me near that pigpen, even though the dawn was breaking and in broad daylight I was sure to be caught and killed.

Only someone who has endured such experiences, hour after hour, day after day, month after month, is able to appreciate the wonder of it all when, later on the road of my suffering, I came upon the camp established by Oskar Schindler, a successful German businessman who nevertheless treated the Jews working for him benignly and tried to make life as bearable as possible within the limitations of a concentration camp.

132

The deeds of Oskar Schindler, who has been recognized as one of the "Righteous Among the Nations," are described in Thomas Keneally's book, *Schindler's List,* (Penguin, 1983). It is thanks once again to the initiative of a single individual that twelve hundred Jews were saved from almost certain death. It is due to Oskar Schindler that I myself survived.

Moshe Bejski is a Justice of the Supreme Court of the State of Israel. Judge Bejski is chairman of the Committee for the Designation of the Righteous at Yad Vashem in Jerusalem.

TEN
QUESTIONS

PIERRE SAUVAGE

One day, 50 years ago, a young French pastor arrived with his wife and children in what seemed to these cosmopolitan city people a rather sleepy mountain community.

The new parish had, however, one promising feature. The pastor, André Trocmé, in a letter to an American friend, dated September 19, 1934, described the village of Le Chambon in France:

> **Here, the old Huguenot spirit is alive. The humblest peasant home has its Bible, and the father reads it every day. So these people, who do not read the papers but the Scriptures, do not stand on the moving soil of opinion but on the rock of the Word of God.**

Time would soon prove just how right he was. Le Chambon has affected my life twice, and I am no longer certain which of the two times is the more important.

It was in Le Chambon that I was born, in March 1944, a Jewish baby, lucky to see the light of day in a place on earth singularly committed to his survival at the very time when much of my family was disappearing into the abyss.

But it is only in the last few years that I have come to sense, in my bones and in my soul, the importance of what the people of Le Chambon, and others like them, can tell us about ourselves, if only we can learn to listen, if only we can recognize our need to listen. Above all, what I have learned so far is that we need to know about the Righteous Gentiles during the Holocaust far more than they need our gratitude.

I shall ask ten questions about the people of Le Chambon and other rescuers of Jews during the Holocaust, questions that suggest ten areas of interdisciplinary, interreligious research and reflection:

1. Virtually all of the people of the area of Le Chambon consider themselves committed Christians. Most of them are the descendents of the Huguenots who fled to this windswept, wintry plateau in the mountains of south-central France so that they might continue practicing their own brand of Christianity without persecution by the kings and Catholics of France.

Aristotle asserts that the true nature of anything is the highest form it can become. But, for a Jew, that is a particularly difficult criterion to apply to Christianity during the Holocaust. The Holocaust occurred in the heart of Christian Europe, and would not have been possible without the apathy or complicity of most Christians and without the virulent tradition of anti-Semitism that had long infected the very soul of Christianity. Are we to view these Christians of Le Chambon, and other caring Christians of that time, as rare but representative of an exemplary Christian faith, or merely as marginal, possibly accidental successes of an otherwise disastrously ineffective one? To summarize, just how Christian were they?

2. However much psychologists, social scientists, and traumatized secular Jews, like me, wish to minimize the spiritual and religious—and hence not scientifically accessible—dimensions of righteous conduct during the Holocaust, the evidence will inevitably generate fundamental questions about the essential nature and specific characteristics of the religious faith of the righteous Christians.

What were their distinctive religious attitudes and perceptions? What did the peasants and villagers of Le Chambon understand that so tragically eluded their Christian brethren from the pope on down?

Could it be, for instance, that the righteous Christians were exceptionally comfortable with the Jewish roots of their faith, indeed, with the Jewishness of Jesus? For them, was Christianity perhaps more the religion *of* Jesus than the religion *about* Jesus?

This appears to have been the remarkable case in Le Chambon. Many Jews never got over their astonishment at being not only sheltered but welcomed as the "people of God," in a place where even their practice of Judaism was protected to some extent.

3. Both André Trocmé and Assistant Pastor Edouard Theis were determined pacifists. On the very day after the armistice with Nazi Germany was signed, they proclaimed during Sunday services that the responsibility of Christians is to resist through the weapons of the spirit the violence that is brought to bear on their consciences.

What can we learn from the dramatic effectiveness of these "weapons of the spirit" in Le Chambon?

If it is true, as the American Roman Catholic bishops proclaimed in their important "Pastoral Letter on War and Peace" that "nonviolent means of resistance to evil deserve much more study and consideration than they have thus far received," should we not begin with the obvious examples of Le Chambon and the

Righteous Gentiles of the Nazi era, including a number of caring, devout Catholics—in whom the Church thus far has shown very little interest?

And to my fellow Jews, I would also like to ask this: Independent even of our share of responsibility in the survival of humankind in this most perilous time in history, do we not have a special incentive to be interested in the *only* weapons that were specifically and productively used by others at that time to save some of us?

Pierre Sauvage was born March 1944, in a peasant house like this at Le Chambon.

4. In Le Chambon, as elsewhere, women played a key role in rescue. It was often women who were faced with the initial all-important decisions as to whether or not to take a stranger into their kitchens and into their homes, a stranger whose presence could imperil the lives of their families. Certainly, the women of Le Chambon were the backbone of much of what occurred there. Could it be that one reason we have been taught so little about Righteous Gentiles is that so-called higher education is dominated by distorting, conventional male values? Is it

easier for male historians to get excited over the sometimes meaningless clatter of military hardware than to get excited about manifestations of spiritual resistance, even when this resistance produced much more tangible results?

Do conventional male values limit our perspective on resistance during the Holocaust?

5. The people of Le Chambon, as Protestants in a Catholic country, were no doubt especially sensitive to the oppression of minorities, and I hasten to add the Catholics of Le Chambon, a minority within a minority, joined actively in the rescue effort. Just how important, just how determinant of the active empathy that developed was this sense of being a minority? Is not every single one of us a minority of one sort or another? And could it be that many of the Righteous Gentiles had a greater sense of this, even before they joined the tiny minority of people who resisted the persecution of the Jews?

6. The moment I became interested in righteous conduct, I had to start rethinking my vocabulary. I am hardly enthusiastic about using the word "righteous" in English, for instance, given that too many people hear "self-righteous" instead. Even the word "gentile" suggests an emphasis on unintended "otherness." I'm interested in righteous people and righteous conduct, not in non-Jews per se. (I also do not like the inadvertent implication that there weren't some equally remarkable Jews acting on similar values and about whom, incidentally, we know even less than about the gentiles.)

But words such as "righteous" and "gentile" appear unavoidable at this stage, and perhaps they can be shaped to meet our needs. Other words, however, are dangerous and must be jettisoned. Just one example that I believe raises a crucial issue is the adjective "selfless," which precludes any understanding of the people it is misleadingly used to praise. I am among those who suspect that Hitler and Eichmann suffered from what could be called a particularly dreadful form of "selflessness," but that could not be said of the people of Le Chambon.

If, indeed, it is true that the people of Le Chambon and elsewhere had a very secure, very anchored sense of self, a spontaneous access to the core of their being, that resulted in a natural and irresistible proclivity to see the truth and act upon it, and if it is indeed true that many or all of the Righteous Gentiles of the Holocaust displayed the characteristic of psychological solidity, then a question arises that my wife and I face all the time as we raise our young son: How does one nurture that powerful and benevolent sense of self-esteem?

If self-esteem was indeed a characteristic of the Righteous, what was special about their upbringing that they succeeded in developing it?

7. It is a rare Righteous Gentile who believes that there was something remarkable about his or her own courage. The people of Le Chambon, through their individual and collective actions, endangered the lives of each and every one of them. Yet, there, too, the risks are acknowledged but not considered to have been a critical part of the decision-making process. We tend to interpret this, and indeed dismiss it, as modesty. But could it be that everybody, except the courageous themselves, attaches more importance to courage than is warranted? Could it be that whenever we overemphasize the courage of the righteous, we do not communicate anything about its nature or help to encourage its emergence?

The town square at Le Chambon.

A glib reference to the courageous, selfless people of Le Chambon may thus have a hollow ring to our ears and generate no real responsiveness in these people, because such words correspond to an empty concept. Perhaps the subconscious intent of such vocabulary is in fact to make such people seem essentially different from you and me, and thus not really, not challengingly, relevant to our daily lives.

How do we learn to view the people of Le Chambon, and others like them, as people with a solid, productive grasp on life, and not as incarnations of fairy-tale virtues which we can then preach about and/or ignore?

8. The people of Le Chambon remember a lot about their heritage and about other important things as well. The people of Le Chambon were well acquainted with the Bible—including the part that Christians designate as the Old Testament, which is, among other things, an exaltation of memory. Just how important is memory in the genesis of righteous conduct? I might ask, in passing, how much do we Americans remember how many of our ancestors came here to escape oppression of one sort or another? And perhaps if Americans had remembered better the oppression of the native Americans and the almost-unfathomable viciousness of slavery, the State Department would have been pressured into helping the persecuted of Europe, instead of being allowed to slam the door on them. Were all havens of refuge for Jews during the Holocaust really havens of the memory of oppression, just as in Le Chambon?

9. Traditional, hierarchical leadership was largely absent among Christians when it came to resisting the appeal of Nazism. But is it not true that we have only the leaders that we deserve? And should we be so hasty as to disregard the possibility that leaders of an untraditional sort may have emerged during that time and that what happens in such situations may be, at least in part, a matter of whether we are capable of recognizing untraditional leaders? We must learn to recognize leaders in a time of moral decay and we should study the forms that their leadership takes.

What sort of leaders did the dynamics of collective rescue produce in Le Chambon and what can we learn about humane leadership from the remarkable effectiveness of André and Magda Trocmé?

10. It appears that the people of Le Chambon often did not know about the rescue efforts their neighbors were making. They barely, if ever, talked about it at the time or after the war when the Jews left. Although there certainly were some overtly collective actions undertaken in the area, the conspiracy of goodness that occurred was, in important respects, a tacit and unspoken one. One might say there was a minyan in Le Chambon. To my knowledge an instance of communal righteousness like this did not occur on this scale, for this length of time, anywhere else in occupied Europe.

Did it result from these persons placing their trust in the beneficence of collective responsibility or from their understanding that this can only occur when there is individual responsibility that starts with oneself?

And since that probably is merely a rhetorical question, let me ask this: If both individual and collective responsibility begin with the notion that it is indeed better to light one candle than to curse the darkness, then how do they ultimately differ?

Albert Camus, whose allegorical novel, *The Plague,* was conceived and begun in the area of Le Chambon has his narrator say this:

> There always comes a time in history when the man who dares to say that two plus two equals four is punished with death....And the issue is not a matter of what reward or what punishment will be the outcome of that reasoning. The issue is simply whether or not two plus two equals four. For those of our townspeople who were then risking their lives, the decision they had to make was simply whether or not they were in the midst of a plague and whether or not it was necessary to struggle against it.

The challenge for us now is to learn to understand the banality of goodness, even during the Holocaust—and to recognize that to care about other people is also to care about yourself.

Pierre Sauvage was born in Le Chambon-sur-Lignon a few months before the end of the German occupation of France. He is president of the Friends of Le Chambon and now lives in California, where he is working on a film about Le Chambon.

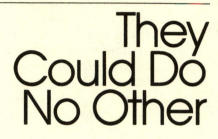

They
Could Do
No Other

ROBERT McAFEE BROWN

As a member of the United States Holocaust Memorial Council, I was privileged to visit Europe in 1979 with other members of the Council, to get ideas for an appropriate Holocaust memorial in the United States. We visited Warsaw and Treblinka, Auschwitz and Birkenau, Kiev and Babi-Yar, and Moscow. Our final destination was Israel.

During the early part of the trip, in both Poland and Russia, we saw monuments, but they were all monuments of dead stone, reminding us of human degradation. In Denmark, however, we encountered monuments of living flesh that testified to the power of human goodness. These were the Danes themselves, those members of the Resistance who, by extraordinary and selfless heroism, reversed the normal experience of Jews in countries occupied by the Nazis. Thanks to these living monuments, 95 percent of Denmark's Jews survived the war.

Why did the Danes side with and shelter Jews, at great risk to themselves, when most of Europe did not? We met with some of them, heroes and heroines now in their seventies and eighties, and asked them why they behaved so nobly. And every time, the reaction was the same: not only did they refuse to be labeled heroes and heroines, they discounted the notion that they had done anything exceptional. Their answer to our question was always to ask another question: "Wouldn't you have helped your neighbors if they had been in trouble?"

And the deeply disturbing thing is that most of us do not know. Would we have tried to save another's life if it had meant risking ours? Most of us, if we are honest, must acknowledge that we become cautious in the face of such a question. When the price can be very high, we search for, and usually find, reasons to excuse ourselves from involvement. The Danes did not.

About three weeks after my return, I received a copy of a then forthcoming book, Philip Hallie's *Lest Innocent Blood Be Shed* (Harper and Row, 1979). So enthralling was it that I read it in a single sitting in a day. I remain grateful for that book, which not only reminded me of the horror of those years, but also highlighted that tiny moment of human splendor that was revealed when the people of the village of Le Chambon-sur-Lignon united at their own risk to save the Jews who needed their help. What struck me in my reading, so soon after the time I had spent in Denmark, was that the people in Le Chambon had reacted in the same way as the Danes: they refused to see anything unusual in what they had done.

The people of Denmark and Le Chambon are not alone in reflecting such an attitude. It seems to have been almost universal among rescuers of Jews during this period. But they are "alone," in the sense that they were atypical of most people confronting similar choices, almost all of whom capitulated to the Nazi mentality toward Jews when forced to choose. Why, then, did a few Europeans see it as a matter of course to risk their lives for Jews, while most, if they ever had such impulses, efficiently curbed them so as not to run afoul of the Nazis?

There are surely times when religion is the dominant motive. Le Chambon's André Trocmé was, after all, a French Reformed pastor, and many who worked fearlessly with him were members of his congregation, people who had learned in their Protestant upbringing that "God alone is Lord of the conscience." In addition, at least some of the Danes must have retained vestiges of the Lutheranism that had informed their national history, and knew well that a time might come when Lutherans, like Luther, might have to say, "Here we stand, we can do no other." Many rescuers in other parts of Europe came from families, or even countries, in which religion was a central feature. During a visit to Poland, for example, I had the privilege of going with Eli Zborowski, a survivor, to visit the Catholic family that had sheltered his family 35 years earlier, and thereby saved their lives. I asked the mother in that home why, in a town and a culture that had little use for Jews, she and her family had taken in the Zborowskis? A simple, unlettered woman, she gave a clear and uncomplicated response: "I do not understand," she said, "why the rest did not hide Jews. We are all Catholics here. How could anyone refuse to hide Jews when our Lord told us that we should help those in need?"

It is a shared resource, then, in the Reformed, Lutheran, and Catholic faiths, and in the Jewish faith as well, that all people, without exception, are made in God's image and therefore must be treated as infinitely precious; they must be afforded whatever protection can be provided by a fellow human being. No other conclusion is possible for those with a true commitment either to God or God's creatures.

It would be comforting if we could stop there and announce the verdict, "case proven." We know, however, that we cannot stop there. The case is not proven, and for two reasons at least. First, there are too many people whose actions on behalf of those in danger spring from other motivations for us to claim that their actions are the result of religious commitment. Second, the overall track record of religious people is abysmally weak; despite the fact that their articles of faith assert that to believe in a just God means to challenge human injustice. More often than not they fail to honor this conviction.

The sad truth is that when we cite instances in which religious faith has led people to protect the weak, we are describing a few brilliant exceptions to the general rule of cowardice or apathy in the face of human need. Those of us who are Christians must remember that we cannot let the few who took risks—the occasional Father Delp, Bishop Lichtenberg, Dietrich Bonhoeffer, or Martin Niemoeller—absolve the rest of us of our failure. St. Paul was not enunciating some complicated doctrine of sin, but merely making a descriptive comment, when he said of himself, in words that describe the rest of us, "The good that I would I do not; the evil that I would not, that I do." (Romans 7:19)

The value, then, of the appeal to religion, in dealing with our question, is that it provides both a way of challenging members of the religious community with the moral yardstick against which they must be measured, and of reminding them (in Johannine terms) that if any persons say they love God but hate their brothers and sisters, they are liars. (1 John 4:20)

So I do not think that religiously inclined people can convincingly offer religion as the full explanation for righteous behavior of those who are not so inclined. "By their fruits you shall know them" (Matthew 7:16) is an awesome and yet justifiable criterion for testing the authenticity of any religious claim. We are to be judged by the quality of our actions rather than by the quantity of our affirmations, by the immediacy of what we do rather than by the intensity of what we say. "Love must not be a matter of words or talk; it must be genuine and show itself in action." (1 John 3:18)

So we need to reflect further on considerations that may lead to righteous behavior. Let me suggest five:

1. It is important to take the disclaiming of heroic deeds seriously. Such statements may be less an instance of false humility than true indications about those who make them. For some people, it may be that the ingrained habits of a lifetime do make it "easy" for them to do what others will not. We need to reflect on the biographies of those who, for whatever reasons, did rise to heights of selflessness to a degree that most did not.

2. Does not involvement in the life of a community of like-minded people render exceptional actions more likely? It is hard as an individual to initiate and maintain

actions that go against the accepted mores of one's society. If there are others involved, taking similar stands, it may sometimes be easier for individuals or minority groups to defy the prevailing wisdom of the majority. This communal support surely helped both the Danes and those in Le Chambon.

3. Those who took risks were, by and large, ordinary people. The comment is not made demeaningly, but as a source of encouragement. The evidence is that the

A deportation in Lodz, Poland.

instinct for love ran deep in unexpected places, and was present not only among leaders or highly gifted people. We need to reflect on the fact that there may be more potential for disinterested action on behalf of others than we usually assume.

4. In addition, however, we may find a further clue to selfless action in the presence of role models for the initially timid. The people of Le Chambon had André Trocmé, providing an example they could not ignore. Trocmé himself had Kindler, the German soldier he met during World War I who was a conscientious objector, as well as Jesus of Nazareth. Martin Luther King had Gandhi. And who knows how many black children, whose names we will never know, had the

146

courage to suffer in the civil rights struggles of the sixties because King himself was their model?

5. These questions deserve fuller treatment than is possible here, but even in this brief presentation it is clear that they pose another question for all of us: Is it not a part of our own obligation today to anticipate crises, to try to determine ahead of time how we wish to act in an emergency?

We should at least be clear that certain attitudes and actions are to be ruled out, come what may—informing on innocent people or being craven before the perpetrators of injustice in the hope of salvaging something for ourselves.

We can at least anticipate a spectrum of possible responses and begin to train ourselves in the discipline necessary to carry them out. One of our main resources will surely be to continue listening to stories from the Nazi era in which ordinary people like ourselves did rise to heroic actions, stories that confront us as well as their participants with the necessity of moral choice and empower us to deal with our own dilemmas by letting us live through the decisions that others had to make for themselves. In this way we can prepare ourselves for the challenges, whether routine or extraordinary, that lie ahead, so that we may act against injustice and inhumanity, and for justice and humanity in whatever situations we find ourselves.

Robert McAfee Brown is a member of the United States Holocaust Memorial Council. He is an author, teacher, and theologian who has written many articles and books, including Elie Wiesel: Messenger to All Humanity *(University of Notre Dame Press, 1983).*

The
Courage
to Care

SHLOMO BREZNITZ

Courage is never alone, for it has fear as its ever-present companion. An act deserves to be called courageous if, and only if, it is performed in spite of fear. The greater the fear, the more courageous the action that defies it. Thus, it is only when fear and anxiety rule supreme that courage can truly assert itself.

But how is it possible to act on a decent principle? How can one expect to overcome the urge for self-protection and safety? And why should a person wish to do so in the first place? Emotions are often viewed as the supreme cause of the condition in which we lose control over our activities. Overwhelmed by the powerful physiological changes that accompany an emotional arousal, we are thought to be at the mercy of what has come over us. Emotions are considered a perfect excuse for a total abdication of responsibility.

In view of its major evolutionary function as the guardian of self-preservation, fear occupies a unique position among all the emotions. It is by virtue of fear, so goes the argument, that our species, just like its predecessors, managed to escape and avoid at least some of "the slings and arrows of outrageous fortune." This was accomplished by ancient biological structures, which never fail to respond with major physiological changes to a serious environmental threat. The racing heart and the shortness of breath guarantee that when faced with adversity, the dry and bitter taste of fear will always play an important role in determining our actions: an important role, yes; total determination, no.

Here, now, is the crux of the matter, for although we often experience the tyranny of fear, we are not forced to be its slaves. It is the difference between the two possible reactions to fear which opens for members of our species a variety of noble opportunities to transcend our evolutionary bondage. The story of primate evolution is the story of attempts at emancipation from the omnipotence of reflexes and instincts. It is a story of transition from automatic responses to behavioral choices, from undifferentiated unanimity to the emergence of individual differences, from dull brute masses to persons.

The attempts of cultures to forge a homo sapiens more free to control his or her destiny are, however, still too fragile to withstand a major assault from the ever-present primitive core. And nothing testifies to this inherent vulnerability of ours in as clear and frightening a manner as the regression of humankind during the Nazi era.

Cultural progress is a precariously weak enterprise that must be cherished and protected at all times. The view which considers emotions solely as unavoidable and uncontrollable outcomes of the provocation of external circumstances is, however, becoming increasingly untenable. Evidence from psychological research suggests that emotions are at least partially determined by the manner in which individuals appraise a given situation. Thus, we can no longer be seen as the passive prisoners of external events. The way we feel and experience the world is to some extent determined by ourselves.

Men and women are not yet full masters of themselves, but internal causes pertaining to their history, attitudes, and moral upbringing are perhaps as important in determining their actions as objective threats and challenges are. This opens vast opportunities, matched only by the increase of personal responsibility for one's actions. Although psychiatry rightly teaches that nobody can stand in judgment of those stricken by fears and anxieties, when we experience fear and anger and love, it is *our* fear and *our* anger and *our* love. And, by far more important, our acts in the face of these emotions have all received our own stamp of approval.

Now we have reached the stuff that courage is made of. It is when fear dictates, "Run," and the mind dictates, "Stay"; when the body dictates, "Don't," and the soul dictates, "Do," that the heroic battle is being waged. At times, for an all-decisive split second, one musters the strength to force the issue; at other times, the difficult decision must be upheld for a long time against renewed attacks of fear and doubt. A short poem by an anonymous soldier which was found on a scrap of paper in a desert trench illustrates this:

> **Stay with me, God. The night is dark,**
> **The night is cold: my little spark**
> **Of courage dies. The night is long;**
> **Be with me, God, and make me strong.**
> **—*Poems from the Desert, 1944***

Courageous acts are often quick and short, as they are in the heat of battle. They are single acts of extreme import, and then the crisis is over. If the individual survives, the next reactions are of relief, vindication, and even, perhaps, gratitude and glory. How, then, can we understand acts that had to be sustained, against all odds, not for seconds or minutes or hours, but days and weeks and months and years? And where? In the midst of the most evil of all empires. And when? During the darkest of all ages.

I have mentioned two measures of courage: the intensity of fear that one has to overcome and the length of time involved. Both are forces against performing a courageous act. With all due caution, I now want to suggest two additional, closely related measures that involve the forces for carrying the act to its completion.

A brave act, by definition, implies risk taking. The issue to consider is, for whose sake is the risk taken? Is it for the sake of the individual himself or herself, a close relative, a dear friend, or is it a commitment to one's group or society? The more distant and intangible the cause, the greater the courage implied by the action. At the farthest extreme of motivation we find those who do not act for themselves or for their close kin, but, like Emile Zola, for the sake of an abstract idea.

I maintain that there is even something more courageous than that. It is when one human being risks everything in order to help save another human being who has been hunted down, degraded, and abandoned by all. As the great poet John Donne wrote:

> No man is an Island entire of itself;
> Every man is a piece of the Continent, a part of the maine;
> If a Clod be washed away by the Sea, Europe is the less,
> as well as if a Promontorie were,
> as well as if a Manor of thy friends or thine own were;
> any man's death diminishes me because I am involved in Mankind;
> And therefore never send to know for whom the bell tolls;
> It tolls for thee.

Last, but not least, there is the issue of expected outcomes. In the midst of the hopelessly unfair battle between fear and courage, one can use any argument, any thought, any image available to bolster one's yet shaky attempts to gain the upper hand. Whether the arguments involve a sense of loyalty, anticipated support from friends and relatives, or images of gratitude, and however weak the arguments are, they are all indispensable. The Righteous Gentiles, however, had to do without it all. As in the highest level of charity (described by the great thinker Rambam), they had to act without anticipation of any reward or acknowledgment. Furthermore, there was a need to maintain secrecy and silence, so that the only source of support they had was from within, from their own commitment and strengths.

Next, consider the alternatives to risking everything for what some could easily perceive as so little. They could have protested, "True, I saw someone in need and did not help. So what? There is a war raging, and thousands of innocent people are dying daily. Why me? And why now?" You see, there is a good reason to believe that after a while the declining of help would at best remain an unpleasant memory, to be conveniently repressed from consciousness at the first opportune moment. Only a few could do better than that; thus, only a few of us were saved. Those that lived up to the occasion discovered that their reward was in the act itself, carried out in "a still and silent voice." Life shrinks or expands in proportion to one's courage. On March 7, 1944, Anne Frank wrote in her diary, "Whoever is happy will make others happy, too. He who has courage and faith will never perish in misery." Let us take these loving words as our beacon of hope. We will be forever grateful to those who refused to let the light fail.

Shlomo Breznitz, a survivor of the Holocaust, lives in Israel where he is professor of psychology at Haifa University.

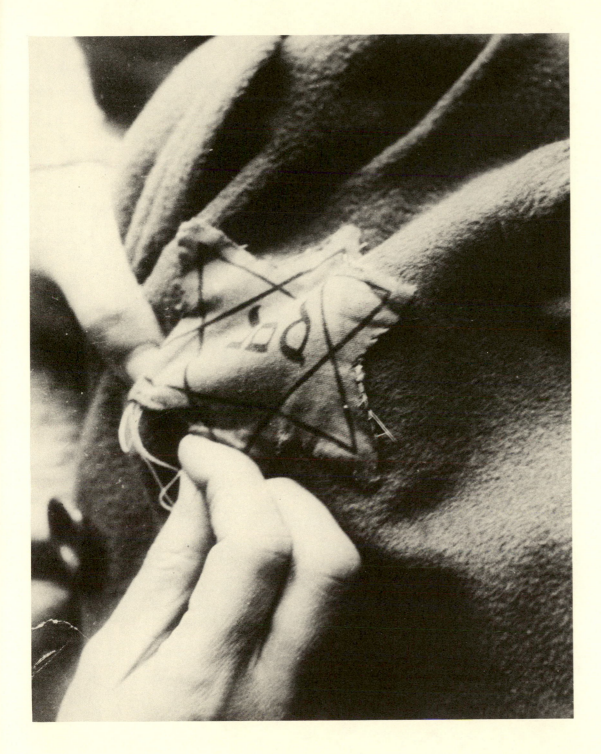

"*Courage is never alone, for it has fear as its ever-present companion. An act deserves to be called courageous if, and only if, it is performed in spite of fear. The greater the fear, the more courageous the action that defies it. Thus, it is only when fear and anxiety rule supreme that courage can truly assert itself.*"

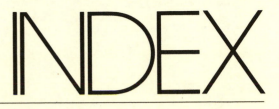